AP® English Language and Literature

2020 online

Erica L. Meltzer

THE CRITICAL READER
New York

Cover by Tugboat Design

ISBN-13: 978-1-7335895-5-0

ALSO BY ERICA MELTZER

The Ultimate Guide to SAT® Grammar & Workbook

SAT® Vocabulary: A New Approach (with Larry Krieger)

The Critical Reader: The Complete Guide to SAT® Reading

The Critical Reader: AP® English Language and Composition Edition

The Complete Guide to ACT® English

The Complete Guide to ACT® Reading

The Complete GMAT® Sentence Correction Guide

GRE® Vocabulary in Practice

How to Write for Class: A Student's Guide to Grammar, Punctuation, and Style

Table of Contents

AP® English Language and Composition

AP® English Literature and Composition

AP English Language and Composition

The Rhetorical Analysis Essay

A [rhetorical analysis] is like a tour of a site or monument; you must accompany the reader, signal the points of interest, and provide clarification that improves his or her understanding of the text.

-Guy Spielmann, Georgetown University

Imagine that you're visiting a college for the first time. You don't know that much about it, but you've heard it has some good programs, and you're thinking of applying. The campus seems nice, and by the time you arrive at the admissions office, you're getting excited.

As soon as you set out on your tour, however, it's clear that the guide is a disaster. He doesn't seem to know which buildings to take you to, or what order he's supposed to show them in, and he doesn't seem to have that much to say about them either. He just stops, mumbles a few vague things, and moves on. When he tries to walk backwards, he stumbles. (How, you wonder, did he ever get hired to represent the school?)

Now imagine the opposite scenario: your guide greets you cheerfully by name. He's smooth and charming, and he talks enthusiastically about his classes and his roommates. He knows exactly where to take you and how much time to spend talking, and he's clear and specific when talking about the school's history and traditions. Moreover, his ability to walk backwards while recounting anecdotes about the university is *outstanding*.

Now tell me: which guide would you want? Presumably, the second.

When you write the rhetorical essay, your goal is essentially to be that second guide. (It could even be argued that doing this type of analysis well is the literary equivalent of walking backwards.)

Now granted, the analogy isn't exact: you will, of course, be analyzing a text you've just seen for the first time rather than a school that you already know something about. But that aside, it largely holds. **In your Rhetorical Analysis Essay—the sole, 45-minute question on the 2020 AP® English Language and Composition exam—your job is to structure your presentation in a clear and logical way so that your reader understands just what is interesting about the text, and how exactly its component parts work together to convey a particular idea for its intended audience.**

Source Texts

Traditionally, the texts used for the Rhetorical Analysis Essay were challenging eighteenth-, nineteenth-, or twentieth-century pieces with substantial rhetorical/stylistic variety and complexity. Since the course description was revised for the 2014-15 school year, however, there has been a noticeable reduction of the complexity of the source texts. So far, the exams administered since 2015 have all included mid-to-late-twentieth-century essays and speeches that are notably less challenging and rhetorically varied than the pre-2015 source texts.

For example, the following excerpt is taken from the 2014 text, an Abigail Adams letter composed in 1780:

> These are times in which a genius would wish to live. It is not in the still calm of life, or the repose of a pacific station, that great characters are formed. Would Cicero have shone so distinguished an orator if he had not been roused, kindled, and inflamed by the tyranny of Catiline, Verres, and Mark Anthony? The habits of a vigorous mind are formed in contending with difficulties. All history will convince you of this, and that wisdom and penetration are the fruit of experience, not the lessons of retirement and leisure.

And here is an excerpt from the 2017 text, a 1960 speech delivered by Clare Boothe Luce to the Women's National Press Club:

> But you are an audience of journalists. There is no audience anywhere who should be more bored— indeed, more revolted — by a speaker who tried to fawn on it, butter it up, exaggerate its virtues, play down its faults, and who would more quickly see through any attempt to do so. I ask you only to remember that I am not a volunteer for this subject tonight. You asked for it!
>
> (https://apcentral.collegeboard.org/courses/ap-english-language-and-composition/exam?course=ap-english-language-and-composition)

It is entirely possible, however, that future tests will contain more challenging sources, so you should be prepared to analyze texts at a range of levels.

In terms of scoring, the College Board is also now downplaying the importance of discussing specific rhetorical figures for the sake of doing so. Instead, it is emphasizing discussion of the source text in terms of the writer's intention to produce a particular reaction, or course of action, from the audience. Note that the assignment asks you to analyze the rhetorical *choices*, not the rhetorical *devices*. It's a subtle but significant choice of words.

In reality, of course, those two things are not easily separated: rhetorical figures are one of the primary means by which a text achieves its effectiveness. Although nearly every text employs some type of rhetorical device, not all texts are equally well written or equally powerful—the difference lies in the style, and you most certainly will not be penalized for providing a detailed analysis that discusses relevant rhetorical figures. That said, you can also focus on more general considerations of how an author achieves a given purpose. (We'll look at some examples in a little while.) And you are also free to bring in your own background knowledge if it happens to be relevant.

Scoring

Essays are scored by trained readers (primarily high school English teachers and college English professors). **The rubric awards points in three main categories, with possible total scores ranging from 0 (lowest) to 6 (highest).**

Thesis: 0-1 point

This is the most straightforward and objective of the three main criteria: having a clear thesis earns you one point; not having a clear thesis gets you no points.

Note, however, that it is almost impossible to earn a zero for the thesis while obtaining the maximum number of points in the other categories—by definition, an essay that lacks a clear thesis will be very difficult to support or argue in a sophisticated way.

1 - There is a clear, defensible thesis that takes a <u>specific position</u> on the prompt.

0 - The thesis is either absent, restates/rewords the prompt without taking a specific position, or extremely vague (e.g., it states that there are pros/cons to both sides of the argument but does not indicate which side the writer agrees with).

The thesis can appear anywhere in your essay—that is, it does not need to be placed at the end of the first paragraph in order to earn the point. In most cases, however, placing it near the beginning will help to keep your essay focused and on-topic.

The thesis may also consist of more than one sentence, provided that the sentences are placed near each other and convey a coherent argument.

Evidence and Commentary: 0-4 points

These points are awarded based on how effectively you support your argument, and on the depth of your analyses and explanations.

4 - Essays that earn a top score provide specific evidence or explanations for each claim; they also make clear how evidence/explanations support the various claims so that the reader is able to follow the logic of the argument. They also explain how specific words and phrases support the writer's argument. **Note that essays with serious grammatical errors cannot earn a 4.**

3 - Essays that earn a 3 demonstrate many of the same qualities as "4" essays but do not provide specific evidence or explanations for all claims and/or do not make (fully) clear how evidence supports arguments or claims.

2 - Essays that earn a 2 fail to provide specific evidence or explain reasoning inconsistently. They may also include information that is off-topic or does not support claims.

1 - Essays that earn a 1 make general claims rather than provide specific evidence and summarize evidence rather than explaining how it supports a claim.

0 - Essays that earn a 0 restate the thesis/information from the sources, or are off-topic.

Sophistication: 0-1 point

This is the most "open" of the three categories, and there are multiple ways to earn the single point it offers.

1 - This point can be earned for either the strength of the writing (e.g., precise and colorful vocabulary, varied sentence structure and punctuation, clear transitions) or the analyses (providing broader context for an argument, acknowledging counterarguments, discussing limitations of an argument).

0 - Essays that earn a 0 in this category contain none of the features necessary for a 1.

Note that this point for sophistication is awarded based on an overall impression of engagement with the prompt and cannot be earned by including a simple phrase, e.g., *Some misguided people believe that x is not true, but such individuals are wrong* (to indicate a counterargument), in an essay that is otherwise very simplistic.

If you are concerned about essay scoring, keep in mind that the readers do take effort into account and are encouraged to give you the benefit of the doubt. They are not looking for excuses to mark you down but rather want you to do well. Moreover, they are explicitly instructed to take into account that the essays are first drafts written under intense time pressure, and to assess them accordingly.

Although you may be most comfortable with the five-paragraph format and are free to use it if you wish, this structure is not required, and there is no particular advantage to organizing your essay that way. Rather than fit your ideas into a rigid, predetermined structure, you are free to choose the organization that best suits your argument.

Note: As of the end of April, College Board has not indicated how scores will be translated from the 6-point essay rubric to the 5-point overall scale. As a result, you should simply focus on writing the strongest essay possible under the given circumstances.

Two general points to keep in mind:

1) Score Correlates with Length

Generally speaking, longer essays tend to receive higher scores. More writing = more in-depth analysis. That said, **correlation is not causation**: An essay that is poorly structured, repetitive, and illogical will not receive a high score, regardless of how much you write.

2) Begin and End on a Strong Note

You get only one chance to make a first impression; readers' minds, once made up, can be hard to change, particularly if an essay is on the border between two scores. Readers cannot devote too much time to each essay and will inevitably start to skim. That said, even if you go slightly off course, having a strong, clear ending that ties things together will give an overall impression of coherence and make any minor issues more likely to be forgiven.

The Main Point

In addition to striking language and punctuation (more about that in a little bit) you should be looking for two main things as you read the passage:

- The main point
- The tone (positive or negative)

The point of a passage is the **primary idea** that the author wants to convey, and along with the topic and the tone, it is the most important thing to look for when you begin to read a passage.

Focusing on finding the point means you don't have a chance to get bored. It reduces the chance that you'll spend five minutes trying to absorb three lines while losing sight of the big idea that really counts. And it stops you from wasting time and energy trying to convince yourself that a passage is interesting when you're actually bored out of your mind.

For the sake of thoroughness, let's start by looking at what a main point is **not**:

- It is not a **topic** such as "the press" or "changes in language" or "class structure."

- It is not a **theme** such as "people vs. nature" or "overcoming oppression."

Topics and themes will get you nowhere; instead, you need to know what the author *thinks*.

A main point is an **argument** that answers the question "so what"? It tells us *why* the author thinks the topic is important, or what essential information he or she wants to convey.

The main point can be thought of in terms of the following formula:

Topic + So What (why does the author care?) = Main Point

Sometimes the author will directly state the main point in the passage itself. If this is the case, you should **underline it immediately**. If not, you need to **write it yourself, in as few words as you can manage**: aim for 3-6. Any more than that and you'll start to get lost in the details.

For example, the main points of some recent exam passages could be summed up as follows:

- 2019, "Gandhi" passage: Non-violent protest worth it
https://apcentral.collegeboard.org/pdf/ap19-frq-english-language.pdf?course=ap-english-language-and-composition

- 2018, Madeleine Albright speech: Must keep promoting women's rights
https://secure-media.collegeboard.org/apc/ap18-frq-english-language.pdf

- 2017: U.S. press = great!
https://apcentral.collegeboard.org/pdf/ap-english-language-frq-2017.pdf?course=ap-english-language-and-composition

How to Read the Passage

As a rule, you should read the passage as quickly as you can while still absorbing the content, making sure to focus on the parts you do understand and not wasting time puzzling over confusing details. It is usually unnecessary to read every word in order to determine the point. Rather, a couple of key places often provide sufficient information: **the main point itself is most often found at either the end of the first paragraph or the beginning of the second paragraph, and then reiterated at the end of the conclusion.**

If you have excellent comprehension and are strong at identifying and summarizing arguments, you should read the passage slowly until you figure out the point; then read the first (topic) and last sentence of each paragraph carefully, skimming through the body of each paragraph and circling major transitions/strong language/interesting punctuation; and read the conclusion carefully, focusing particularly on and <u>underlining</u> the last sentence or two because the main point will often be restated there.

Reading this way will allow you to create a mental "map" of how the passage is structured: the introduction and conclusion will most likely give you the point of the passage, and each topic sentence will generally provide you with the point of the paragraph, allowing you to understand how it fits into the argument as a whole. Then, when you think about the details, you'll already understand the ideas that they support and have a general sense of the roles that they play within the passage.

Generally speaking, non-fiction authors are pretty clear about the parts of their writing that they want you to pay attention to: if they're really generous, they'll even come right out and tell you what the point is. Even if they're not quite that blatant, however, they usually make a decent effort to tell you what's important.

So first, if the word *important* or any of its synonyms (*essential, crucial, central, key*) appears in the middle of a paragraph as you're racing through, you need to slow down, circle it, and read that part carefully. **If the author says it's important, it's important.** There's no trick.

You must also be able to recognize when an argument changes or when new and important information is being introduced: transitions such as *however, therefore, in fact;* "unusual" punctuation such as italics (used for emphasis), dashes and colons (used to signal explanations); and strong language such as *only, never,* and *extremely* are all "clues" that tell you to pay attention. Note that as a general rule, you should avoid circling nouns (with the exception of words like *reason, explanation,* and *problem*) because they do not tell you why particular pieces of information are important.

One important step that you should make sure not to forget is to **read the blurb before the passage**! It will always provide important contextual information about the original purpose of and audience for the passage—information that you must take into account when considering why the writer makes the particular set of rhetorical decisions that he or she makes. Indirectly (or sometimes more directly), the blurb also essentially tells you the point of the passage, making your job significantly easier.

Paradoxically, you may also want to begin by reading the end of the passage. If you already know where the author is heading, you can view his or her choices in the beginning and middle in light of that specific goal.

Functions of Key Words, Transitions, and Punctuation

Continuers

Support, Illustrate, Bolster, Provide Evidence

Also
And
As well as
Furthermore
For example
For instance
In addition
Moreover
One reason/another reason

Indicate Sequence of Events

First/In the first place
Next
Then
Previously
Subsequently
Finally

Explain, Clarify, Define

Effectively
Essentially
In other words
The answer/reason is
That is
Colon
Dash

Cause and Effect

Accordingly
As a result
As such
Because
Consequently
For
Hence
So
Therefore
Thus
Thereby
To these ends

Compare

Likewise
(Just) as
Much as/like
More/Less…than
Similarly

Define

That is (to say)
Properly speaking
Colon
Dash
Parentheses

Hypothesize, Speculate

If
May
Maybe
Might
Could
Perhaps
It is possible
Would

Emphasize, Highlight, Call Attention to, Underscore

Indeed
In fact
Let me be clear
Italics
Capital letters
Exclamation point
Repetition (of a word, phrase)
Hyperbole (exaggeration)

Indicate Importance

Important
Significant
Essential
Fundamental
Central
Key
The point is

Contradictors

Refute, Criticize, Challenge, Dispute, Contrast

(Al)though/Even though
Alternately/Alternatively
But
Conversely
Despite
However
In contrast
In spite of
Instead
Meanwhile
Nevertheless
On the contrary
On one hand/On the other hand
Otherwise
Still
Regardless
Rather than
Whereas
While
Yet

Question, Imply Skepticism

But is it really true…?
Question mark
Quotation marks

Qualify

Dashes
Parentheses

Tone and Attitude

Tone and attitude are similar concepts—at the most basic level, both indicate a positive, negative, or neutral stance—but they are not precisely the same thing. Essentially, tone involves specific features of the text, whereas attitude involves emotions.

Generally, the author's—or, more likely, the speaker's—tone and attitude will be directly aligned—that is, they will use clearly positive or negative words and phrases to convey the corresponding attitude. For instance, in the following example from Clare Boothe Luce's 1960 speech to the Women's National Press Club, Luce abruptly shifts from one end of the emotional spectrum to the other, as indicated by the change in her language.

> I am **happy and flattered** to be a guest of honor on this always **exciting** and challenging occasion. But looking over this audience tonight, I am **less happy** than you might think and **more challenged** than you could know.

In this case, the relationship between tone and attitude is clear; in other instances, however, a subtler, more neutral or complex language may be used to convey the speaker's attitude.

> I have **no desire to cause you unnecessary embarrassment,** or any at all, so far as I can **help**. If you think that there is any substance in my letter, and if you will **care** to discuss matters with me, and if to that end you would like me to postpone publication of this letter, **I shall gladly refrain** on receipt of a telegram to that effect soon after this reaches you.

In this case, the challenging language and syntax make the tone of this excerpt (from a 1930 Gandhi speech, 2019 exam) considerably more difficult to determine than in the previous example. If you read carefully, however, you can discern some significant clues: Gandhi does not want to cause the recipient of his letter *unnecessary embarrassment* and, moreover, he is willing not to publish his letter immediately (*if you would like me to postpone publication of this letter*) if its recipient prefers to discuss its contents with him first. Although the tone is relatively restrained in comparison to the previous example, Gandhi's attitude toward the letter's recipient is positive and could be described as "sympathetic."

The chart below lists some common tone/attitude words that can help you improve the specificity of your analyses.

Positive	Negative	Neutral
Appreciative	Critical	Analytical
Approving	Disapproving	Dispassionate
Conversational	Disbelieving	Evenhanded
Humorous	Disdainful	Impartial
Informal	Dismissive	Informative
Optimistic	Disparaging	Measured
Proud	Dubious	Objective
Reverent	Skeptical	Restrained
Sympathetic	Wary	Tempered

Register

Register refers to how **formal** or **informal** a text is. Many Rhetorical Analysis passages are generally written in a tone that ranges from moderately formal (as in the Gandhi example in the previous section) to extremely formal, as in the example below.

> The eye of the reformer is met with angry flashes, portending disastrous times; but his heart may well beat lighter at the thought that America is young, and that she is still in the impressible stage of her existence. May he not hope that high lessons of wisdom, of justice and of truth, will yet give direction to her destiny? Were the nation older, the patriot's heart might be sadder, and the reformer's brow heavier. Its future might be shrouded in gloom, and the hope of its prophets go out in sorrow. There is consolation in the thought that America is young.

This type of tone is often associated with attempts to persuade an audience through logic, or by impressing/inspiring them with elevated, lofty language.

At the other extreme, you may also encounter moments in which an author/speaker adopts a more conversational or even slightly humorous tone. For example, let's return to this excerpt from the Clare Boothe Luce passage.

> But you are an audience of journalists. There is no audience anywhere who should be more bored—indeed, more revolted—by a speaker who tried to fawn on it, butter it up, exaggerate its virtues, play down its faults, and who would more quickly see through any attempt to do so. I ask you only to remember that I am not a volunteer for this subject tonight. **You asked for it!**

Here, the final statement creates a tone that is informal, or conversational. If you do encounter a flash of humor in a passage, make sure to note it. Most likely, the author or speaker is employing it in order to charm the audience, or to gain their interest or confidence.

Point of View

Assuming that the 2020 Rhetorical Analysis passage follows the pattern of the 2017-2019 exams, the text is likely to be excerpted from a political speech. If this is indeed the case, then the passage is likely to be written from either a **first-person** (*I*) or a **second-person** (*you*) perspective. It may also include both points of view, as in the Boothe example above.

If the passage does include any changes in narrative perspective, you should make sure to mark it as you read. It will almost certainly occur at a significant point in the passage and will likely accompany a shift in tone, making it a prime candidate for discussion in your essay.

Counterarguments and Concessions

One common rhetorical strategy that often gets short shrift in high school English classes is the **counterargument**: an idea that goes against the author's argument. Likewise, a **counterexample** is an example that provides support for an opposing point of view. Authors may also respond with a **rebuttal**, in which they push back against an opposing perspective.

Most of the time, authors include counterarguments in order to explain why those arguments are incorrect. However, they may sometimes also cite aspects of an opposing argument with which they *do* agree, or whose validity they recognize. This type of agreement is signaled through the use of **concessions**—that is, **acknowledgements** of the merits of an opposing claim.

Consider, for example, the following excerpt from Frederick Douglass's famous 1852 speech "What to the Slave is the Fourth of July?" in which the speaker, a former slave, explains the bitter irony of Independence Day for him. Before he launches into the main part of his critique, he says the following:

> Fellow Citizens, I am not wanting in respect for the fathers of this republic. The signers of the Declaration of Independence were brave men. They were great men too — great enough to give fame to a great age. It does not often happen to a nation to raise, at one time, such a number of truly great men. **The point from which I am compelled to view them is not, certainly, the most favorable; and yet I cannot contemplate their great deeds with less than admiration.**

Rather than denounce the signers of the Declaration of Independence as hypocrites or oppressors, here Douglass makes a concession by acknowledging that he admires them—even though he has no reason to be sympathetic to them.

In some cases, a counterargument may be implied rather than directly stated, for example in this excerpt from John F. Kennedy's inaugural speech:

> To those people in the huts and villages of half the globe struggling to break the bonds of mass misery, we pledge our best efforts to help them help themselves, for whatever period is required—**not because the communists may be doing it, not because we seek their votes,** but because it is right. If a free society cannot help the many who are poor, it cannot save the few who are rich.

Here, the bolded section is a response to an implied criticism: you are only helping "those people" because the communists are also doing it, or because you want people's votes. The underlined section then serves as the rebuttal, in which Kennedy reasserts his own position: we do these things because they are good in themselves, not for an ulterior motive.

How to Write Your Thesis

Simply put, a thesis is an argument, i.e., the main point: the central claim or assertion that your essay will be devoted to supporting. Note that in terms of the Rhetorical Analysis Essay, you are essentially making an argument about an argument.

To determine your thesis, you can use the following formula: **Topic + So What + How?**

In other words:

- What is the topic of the passage?
- What point about it does the author want to convey?
- What techniques or devices does the author use to convey it?

To be effective, a thesis must be both **specific** and **debatable**. It should NOT:

- Summarize the passage, or state the topic/theme
- Stretch beyond the scope of the passage
- Consist of a statement that is generally recognized as true

Note how each of the "effective" examples below provides a clear and precise argument that limits the scope of the discussion.

Vague:	Throughout her speech, Albright uses several rhetorical techniques to convey her point.
Effective:	Throughout her speech, Albright uses repetition and logos to argue for the continued importance of promoting women's rights on a global scale.
Vague:	In the passage, Gandhi talks about what he believe in his heart is right.
Effective:	In the passage, Gandhi uses understatement and a personal tone to emphasize the effectiveness of nonviolent resistance.
Vague:	In her speech to the Women's National Press Club, Clare Boothe Luce shows that the press is important.
Effective:	In her speech to the Women's National Press Club, Clare Boothe Luce uses varied punctuation and an enthusiastic tone to celebrate the strength of the American press.

To recap, here are some key questions to keep in mind when developing your thesis:

Big-Picture

- Why is the piece being written/delivered?
- Who is the audience?
- Is the author's relationship to that audience positive or negative?
- Does the author want to inspire readers? Move them? Entertain them?

Style

- Is there repetition? Of words? Of phrases?
- Does the author use any strong or extreme language? Where, and to emphasize what idea?
- Are there any big changes in tone or point of view? Where?
- Diction: Every passage contains "diction" (i.e., words)—if you choose to discuss this device, you should be ready to explain what *type* of diction the passage includes.

  What types of words does the author use? Verbs? Adjectives? Is the focus on action or description?

  Does the author use a vocabulary associated with any particular field (e.g., history, economics, sports)? If so, what purpose does it serve?

Organizing Your Essay

Without a clear overall plan, the Rhetorical Analysis Essay can easily become vague, repetitive, and difficult to follow.

There are essentially two main options for organizing a rhetorical strategy essay:

1) By rhetorical device

When you have finished annotating the passage and making note of the various devices it contains, **choose the three most prominent/significant ones, and devote a paragraph to each**. If there is an additional device that seems to demand discussion, you can go to four, but anything beyond that will usually cause your essay to lose focus.

Note that if a text is relatively unvaried rhetorically, or does not contain particularly interesting figures, you are probably better off with Option #2.

2) Chronologically

In this organization, you can trace the evolution of an author's tone or approach throughout the essay, considering how each rhetorical "step" serves a larger purpose or is designed to elicit a particular reaction. Very often, for example, an author will start out in a very modest or understated way and gradually build to a series of strong statements.

In such cases, you can divide the passage into sections, e.g., beginning, middle, and end, and consider the key rhetorical feature(s) of each, explaining how the writer's focus and strategies evolve. In order to stay focused, you should limit yourself to discussing no more than two or three of the most important strategies in each section.

Two additional points to keep in mind:

Perhaps the most common trap that students fall into on the rhetorical essay is to devote too much space to quoting and/or paraphrasing the passage and not enough space to actually commenting on it. To be clear, it is necessary to include plenty of direct citations, but as is true for any essay, it is also necessary to introduce or frame them in such a way that their purpose within your argument is clear. You should also make sure not to jump from point to point without citing and/or commenting on the text sufficiently before moving on.

For example, consider the following paragraph based on the 2015 text by labor leader Cesar Chavez:

> In the fifth paragraph (lines 22-32), Chavez states that "Nonviolence has exactly the opposite effect." The writing is characterized by a mix of short and long sentences, and Chavez also utilizes repetition of the word "we": "We attract people's support" (line 24), "We can gather the support of millions," (lines 24-25), and "we are convinced" (line 27). Chavez also concludes the paragraph with a short sentence, "It is to that yearning that we appeal," (lines 31-32) that contrasts with the two longer, less abrupt sentences that precede it.

Can you spot the problem with this paragraph? Although it provides a description of the text as well as specific examples, we have absolutely no idea what the purpose of those examples *is*. In fact, there is no analysis, just a series of apparently random observations. Although the writing itself is clear and grammatically correct, this type of non-analysis will lead to a lower score in both the "Commentary and Evidence" and "Sophistication" categories.

Now consider this version:

> In the fifth paragraph (lines 22-32), Chavez uses repetition, or anaphora, to create a sense of solidarity with his audience. "<u>We</u> attract people's support" (line 24), "<u>We</u> can gather the support of millions," (lines 24-25), and "<u>we</u> are convinced" (line 27). This repetition of the word "we" serves to create a sense that both Chavez and his readers are partners in the same peaceful approach to resolving conflict. When he repeats that word again in the final sentence of the paragraph (lines 31-32), it is given an additional impact because it appears in a short, direct sentence that contrasts sharply with the longer, less abrupt ones that precede it.

In contrast to the original version, this paragraph has a single, clear focus (repetition of *we* = solidarity) that remains consistent and is developed throughout the paragraph.

A second misconception among students is that they need to bend over backwards talking about how wonderful the author is. In fact, you should take care to avoid such overblown statements as "In her extraordinary essay, author x demonstrates the true depths of her genius...Readers will be overwhelmed by the phenomenal brilliance of her writing." It's fine to point out a particularly clever turn of phrase, or to point out that a writer is using very strong language in order to emphasize a point, but talking about how amazing, extraordinary, etc. a passage is should not be mistaken for actually analyzing it.

The Importance of Making an Outline

In addition to your thesis, you should determine your major points/sections, as well as your examples, and have that information present to refer back to as you write. If you make sure in your outline that 1) your thesis clearly responds to the prompt; 2) each point clearly supports your thesis; and 3) each example clearly illustrates the relevant point, your argument will remain focused throughout the essay.

Indeed, it is almost impossible to overstate the importance of spending a few minutes organizing your thoughts before you begin writing your actual essay. Going off-topic or failing to respond to the specific prompt is a guaranteed way to lose easy points, and having a clear outline will prevent you from falling into that trap.

On the following page, we're going to look at how a rhetorical strategy essay gets constructed. Because adult examples of this type of writing tend to be in very short supply, I am including a sample essay of my own. Two real student essays follow.

On June 5, 1947, United States Secretary of State George C. Marshall delivered the following address at Harvard University's commencement ceremony. Read the following excerpt from the speech carefully. Then, in a well-written essay, analyze the rhetorical choices Marshall makes to **develop his argument about the United States' obligation to help rebuild Europe after World War II**.

I need not tell you that the world situation is very serious. That must be apparent to all intelligent people. I think one difficulty is that the problem is one of such enormous complexity that the very mass facts presented to the public by press and radio make it exceedingly difficult for the man in the street to reach a clear appraisement of the situation. Furthermore, the people of this country are distant from the troubled areas of the earth and it is hard for them to comprehend the plight and consequent reactions of the long-suffering peoples, and the effect of those reactions on their governments in connection with our efforts to promote peace in the world.

In considering the requirements for the rehabilitation of Europe the physical loss of life, the visible destruction of cities, factories, mines and railroads was correctly estimated, but it has become obvious during recent months that this visible destruction was probably less serious than the dislocation of the **entire** fabric of the European economy. For the past ten years conditions have been highly abnormal. The feverish preparation for war and the more feverish maintenance of the war effort engulfed all aspects of national economies. Machinery has fallen into disrepair or is **entirely obsolete**. Long-standing commercial ties, private institutions, banks, insurance companies and shipping companies disappeared, through loss of capital, absorption through nationalization or by simple destruction. In many countries, confidence in the local currency has been **severely** shaken. The breakdown of the business structure of Europe during the war was complete. Recovery has been **seriously retarded** by the fact that two years after the close of hostilities a peace settlement with Germany and Austria has not been agreed upon. **But** even given a more prompt solution of these difficult problems, the **rehabilitation** of the economic structure of Europe quite evidently will require a much longer time and greater effort than had been foreseen.

There is a phase of this matter which is both interesting and serious. The farmer has always produced the foodstuffs to exchange with the city dweller for the other necessities of life. This division of labor is the basis of modern civilization. At the present time it is threatened with breakdown. Governments are forced to use their foreign money and credits to procure necessities abroad. This process exhausts funds which are **urgently** needed for reconstruction.

The truth of the matter is that Europe's requirements for the next three or four years of foreign food and other essential products—principally from America—are so much greater than her present ability to pay that she **must** have substantial additional help, or face economic, social and political deterioration of a very grave character. The remedy lies in breaking the vicious circle and restoring the confidence of the European people in the economic future of their own countries and of Europe as a whole. The manufacturer and the farmer throughout wide areas **must** be able and willing to exchange their products for currencies the continuing value of which is not open to question.

Aside from the demoralizing effect on the world at large and the possibilities of disturbances arising as a result of the desperation of the people concerned, the consequences to the economy of the United States should be apparent to all. It is **logical** that the United States should do whatever it is able to do to assist in the return of normal economic health in the world, without which there can be no political stability and no assured peace. **Our policy** is directed not against any country or doctrine but against hunger, poverty, desperation and chaos. Its purpose should be the revival of a working economy in the world so as to permit the emergence of political and social conditions in which free institutions can exist. Such assistance, I am convinced, must not be on a piece-meal basis as various crises develop. **Any assistance** that this Government may render in the future should provide a cure rather than a mere palliative. **Any government** that is willing to assist in the task of recovery will find full cooperation, I am sure, on the part of the United States Government. **Any government** which maneuvers to block the recovery of other countries cannot expect help from us. Furthermore, governments, political parties or groups which seek to perpetuate human misery in order to profit therefrom politically or otherwise will encounter the opposition of the United States.

Outline

Thesis: Marshall balances appeals to logic and reason with a sense of urgency to persuade audience to adopt his plan.

Intro: Europe in shambles 1947, Marshall Plan necessary to rebuild. Structures appeal so that seriousness of situation is made clear first, then asks f/US help.

Text has 3 parts:

I. First paragraph (1-13): acknowledges audience's hesitations, counterargument, makes more willing to accept argument

II. Lines 14-50: explain how bad Euro. situation is

A. Focus on economics, infrastructure: factories, trade, cities, railroads, etc.

B. Also uses extreme language to convey urgency: entirely, severely…

C. Why present argument this way? B/c talking to Harvard grads + families: influential people, people with power, can legitimize his ideas, make mainstream

III. Lines 51-end

A. Shifts focus to US

B. Vocabulary of sickness/health

C. Ends w/repetition/"Any" – puts burden on US to act.

Concl: Plan was adopted, success, led to rebuilding of Euro economy, stabiliztn

Important:

The following essay was written to provide you with a professional example of a rhetorical analysis so that you can understand the range of strategies and techniques that can be discussed. As a result, it is somewhat longer and more complex than what can typically be produced in the 40 minutes or so allotted for this assignment. **While you may want to use portions of it as models for your own analyses, you do NOT need to produce something comparable to achieve a high score!**

Given the College Board's current emphasis on the relationship between audience/context and text, however, I also have chosen to play up the historical aspect somewhat in order to demonstrate how outside knowledge can be integrated into and inform a discussion of specific textual elements. However, it is **not** necessary to demonstrate significant background knowledge to complete the essay successfully.

Introduction

The introduction serves to introduce and "frame" the topic you are about to discuss. It should be generally consistent with the **scope** of your essay—that is, how broad or narrow it is. The Rhetorical Analysis Essay is always very narrow in scope—even if the passage concerns a broad theme, your response must be written in response to the specific language of that particular text—and your introduction should reflect that fact.

As a result, you should avoid sweeping, overly general openings.

> Throughout history, obedience has been emphasized by society.

Or:

> Since the dawn of human existence, people have rebelled against injustice.

Both of these statements are **far too broad**—your essay is not about obedience since the beginning of time. These types of introductions make your writing seem vague and generic.

For the introduction as a whole, you may find it helpful to use the following simple three-part "formula."

Step 1: Introduce the topic by providing basic context

In 1947, Europe lay in ruins. Two years after the end of World War II, large swathes of countries from France to Germany to Italy remained devastated, their cities and towns destroyed and their populations still often lacking in basic necessities.

Step 2: Transition to the passage

It is against that backdrop that U.S. Secretary of State George C. Marshall's historic 1947 Harvard commencement address must be considered. In the speech, Marshall first outlines the dangers of allowing Europe's situation to fester unchecked and then presents the argument that the United States must step in and aid in Europe's recovery.

Step 4: State your thesis

Throughout the passage, he deftly balances the need to convey the urgency of Europe's plight with a series of calculated appeals to logic that serve to persuade audience members of their country's global responsibility.

In general, you should try to limit your introduction to 5-6 sentences; any longer, and you risk falling into the analysis itself and ending up with a "top-heavy" essay. Given that you will have less than 45 minutes to actually write, your goal should be to give the reader just enough context to follow your argument and then move quickly on to the body of the essay.

Body Paragraphs

Unless there is a compelling reason to make a section shorter, you should aim for at least five sentences in each body paragraph; anything less will not allow sufficient development. Note the consistent use of transitions to keep the reader oriented with the argument.

Step 1: Transition + topic sentence

In the first section (lines 1-13), Marshall begins not by stating his proposal outright **but** by making a concession to the audience's potential concerns—**essentially**, he paves the way for their eventual willingness to consider his plan by recognizing their potential protestations.

Step 2: Introduce example (quotation)

The European problem, he acknowledges, is one of "enormous complexity" (line 4), and "it is hard for [the people of this country] to comprehend the plight and consequent reactions of the long-suffering peoples" (lines 9-11).

Step 3: Analyze the example, tying it back to your thesis

Clearly, Marshall recognizes that from the comparatively privileged vantage point of the United States, the suffering in Europe must seem very foreign indeed. **At the same time**, he subtly flatters his listeners by referring to "all intelligent people" (lines 2-3), implicitly including them in that description.

Do not forget this last step! Directly or indirectly, you must tie your example back to your thesis; do not assume that the reader can put the pieces together. Remember that your goal is to make your argument as easy as possible to follow.

Now let's look at the other body paragraphs in more traditional format:

Having acknowledged the audience's hesitation, Marshall shifts and structures his appeal on logical, pragmatic grounds (lines 14-50). To that end, throughout the second section he cites a variety of concrete problems related to economics and infrastructure, for example the destruction of "cities, factories, mines, and railroads" (lines 16-17), and later, "commercial ties, private institutions, banks" (lines 26-28). As Marshall goes on to explain, the breakdown in the division of labor that is "the basis of modern civilization" (line 45) has the potential to cause an economic catastrophe. Although his tone is fairly restrained, he also takes care to emphasize the severity of the situation: machinery is "entirely obsolete" (lines 25-26); "confidence in the local currency has been severely shaken" (lines 30-31); "recovery has been seriously retarded" (lines 33-34). The repetition of these intensifiers serves to impress upon listeners the extent to which Europe is teetering on the brink of economic collapse. At the same time, Marshall avoids the type of hyperbole that might cause his exceptionally well-educated audience to question him.

In fact, when the audience for the speech is taken into account, this hardheaded appeal to logic makes sense: Marshall is not merely addressing a group of university graduates. Rather, he is addressing a group of Harvard graduates: on the whole, one of the most intellectually accomplished groups in the United States. (It is no coincidence that Marshall alludes to "all intelligent people" in the first line!) It is also a group that exerts a disproportionate influence on American government and culture. Given that context, the focus on economic and technocratic concerns is only natural: it is undoubtedly intended to make the audience more receptive to his words and thus more likely to give his plan the stamp of mainstream approval.

After establishing the severity of the European crisis, Marshall then shifts toward the true purpose of his speech: namely, to explain the United States' responsibility to aid Europe (lines 51-90). Notably, Marshall briefly adopts a slightly more relaxed tone in line 51, opening his appeal by invoking "the truth of the matter." With its somewhat conversational overtones, this phrase gives the sense that Marshall is leveling with the audience, and addressing them with unvarnished honesty. When he then begins to insist openly that the United States has an obligation to provide aid, his words become more forceful. For example, at the beginning of the last paragraph, the use of repetition conveys a sense of urgency and importance: Europe "must have substantial additional help" (line 55); "the manufacturer and the farmer...must be able to exchange their products..." (lines 60-62). He also injects a note of emotional poignancy by alluding to the "desperation" (line 66) of the people.

Notably, in this section, he increasingly employs the vocabulary of sickness and health as well as that of logic, suggesting the United States should essentially play the role of doctor to a "feverish" Europe: words and phrases such as "remedy" (line 57), "normal economic health" (line 70), "a cure rather than a mere palliative" (lines 80-81), and "recovery" (line 85) cast the United States in the role of the "logical" physician, calmly and judiciously dispensing the necessary cure for an ailing patient. It is a metaphor likely to appeal to this most rational of audiences.

As the passage moves towards its conclusion, Marshall's language becomes both stronger and more inclusive. Significantly, in line 72, he refers to "Our policy" rather than to "America" or "The United States." The implication is that the plan is not something to be imposed from above; rather, it is the result of collective decision, one that implicitly includes the audience. In the final lines, he again employs repetition (anaphora) to emphasize the United States' determination to ensure the success of the plan, referring to "Any assistance" (line 79), "Any government" (line 81), and again "Any government which maneuvers to block the recovery of other countries cannot expect help from us" (lines 84-86). Crucially, he ends by invoking "the United States government" (lines 83-84) and "the United States" (lines 89-90) – the onus of responsibility has now been shifted squarely onto his country.

Conclusion

Your conclusion does not need to be particularly long. In general, you can aim for about three sentences—just enough to finish things off without seeming overly abrupt.

Step 1: Transition to conclusion

Ultimately what came to be known as the Marshall Plan was an extraordinary success, on a scale that was perhaps beyond what anyone sitting in Harvard Yard on that June day in 1947 could have imagined.

Step 2: Reiterate thesis and explain larger significance of topic

Marshall's ability to **convey the seriousness of the European situation while appealing to the intellectual bent of his audience** undoubtedly smoothed the way for the adoption of his plan—a plan that helped spur the European post-war economic boom and that, for a time at least, helped reestablish a previously unimaginable level of stability across the continent.

Analysis:

There are a few main things to notice about this essay:

First, it is an example of linear organization. Rather than focusing on three (or more) rhetorical figures of primary importance and devoting a paragraph to each, it traces the development of the passage from beginning to end.

At the same time, however, it does not just consist of a series of disconnected observations: it contains a specific thesis (*Marshall deftly balances the need to convey the urgency of Europe's plight with a series of calculated appeals to logic*), and each part of the essay supports it by pointing out the various ways in which Marshall alternates between these two "poles" in the relevant section of his speech.

In addition, the essay considers Marshall's rhetorical decisions in both general and specific ways. In addition to analyzing the use of tools such as diction (technocratic language and intensifiers) and repetition, it also devotes a full paragraph to examining the relationship between the practical, economic emphasis of the speech and the highly educated audience to which it is directed.

Note also that while the essay discusses diction, it does so in a non-generalized way. Instead, it cites specific types of vocabulary, e.g., "intensifiers" such as *entirely*, *severely*, and *seriously* in the second part of the passage, and vocabulary involving sickness and health in the third part.

Finally, to reiterate: while you are not required to devote so much space to analyzing the relationship between the writer/speaker and his or her audience, you should be prepared to use contextual information provided in the blurb before the passage to at least touch on that question at some point in your essay.

Having considered the big picture, in the next section we're going to look at some general stylistic issues.

Avoid Casual Language

In the Rhetorical Analysis Essay, you are expected to write in the same moderately formal style and follow the same conventions you would use in any paper written for school. Although a couple of minor errors scattered throughout your essay will not affect your score, the presence of repeated and obvious mistakes will prevent you from earning the "Sophistication" point.

Casual: Virginia Woolf's speech "Professions for Women" encourages women to reject **the idea that they can't do stuff**.

Formal: Virginia Woolf's speech "Professions for Women" encourages women to reject **the limits that society places on their ambitions**.

All words should be written out (with the exception of titles that are normally abbreviated, e.g., Dr. and Mr.). Do not use ampersands (& signs) or other abbreviations.

Incorrect: On January 20th, 1961, John F. Kennedy successfully read his inaugural address to a large crowd of Americans **&** became the 35th president.

Correct: On January 20th, 1961, John F. Kennedy successfully read his inaugural address to a large crowd of Americans **and** became the 35th president.

Refer to the author/speaker by their last/full name, not their first name.

Incorrect: In her speech "Professions for Women," **Virginia** encourages women to reject the limits that society places on them and pursue their ambitions.

Correct: In her speech "Professions for Women," **Woolf (or: Virginia Woolf)** encourages women to reject the limits that society places on them and pursue their ambitions.

Use Verbs and Nouns, Not -ING Words (Gerunds)

Another way to strengthen your writing is to avoid the unnecessary use of -ING words (gerunds). Like the passive, this construction can easily become awkward and weigh down your writing.

Awkward: **Because of her having** so much poise and self-regard, Woolf demonstrates that she is worthy of **being a**dmired by other women.

Clearer: **Because she has** so much poise and self-regard, Woolf demonstrates that she is worthy of **being** admired by other women.

Clearest: **Because she has** so much poise and self-regard, Woolf demonstrates that she is worthy of **other women's admiration**.

Tense Consistency

From a stylistic perspective, one surefire way to make a poor impression is to repeatedly switch verb tenses without a clear reason for doing so. What starts in the present should stay in the present, and what starts in the past should stay in the past.

As a general rule, you should use the **literary present** when referring to the source text. You should only use the past tense to discuss events that clearly occurred in the past.

Incorrect: Cesar Chavez's speech **focused** on the necessity of nonviolent protest.

Correct: Cesar Chavez's speech **focuses** on the necessity of nonviolent protest.

BUT:

Incorrect: On December 1, 1955, a Montgomery bus driver ordered Rosa Parks to give up her seat to a white passenger. Parks, already an experienced and committed Civil Rights activist, **refuses** to do so and was promptly arrested.

Correct: On December 1, 1955, a Montgomery bus driver ordered Rosa Parks to give up her seat to a white passenger. Parks, already an experienced and committed Civil Rights activist, **refused** to do so and was promptly arrested.

Using Transitions Effectively

The effective use of transitions is a key factor in achieving a high score. These words and phrases serve as "signposts" that help readers orient themselves in your argument. They indicate whether you are presenting additional evidence, introducing a contrasting example, pointing out causes and effects, or drawing a comparison between one example and the next. From a stylistic perspective, they help you join ideas so that your writing flows smoothly.

Example 1: **Although** Gandhi admits that violence can provide temporary relief or satisfaction, he **also** contends that it causes people and societies an unacceptable amount of suffering.

Example 2: Cesar Chavez's father and uncle were active supporters of unionization; **therefore,** Chavez learned about strikes, organizing operations, and picket lines at a young age.

Example 3: To illustrate the plight of those who suffer because of indifference, **not only** does Wiesel appeal to the audience's conscience **but he also** suggests that society has not learned sufficiently from the past.

Note that one relatively simple way to make your writing sound more sophisticated is to place an occasional transition in the middle of a sentence rather than at the beginning.

Beginning: Gandhi admits that violence can provide temporary relief or satisfaction. **However**, he also contends that it causes people and societies an unacceptable amount of suffering.

Middle: Gandhi admits that violence can provide temporary relief or satisfaction. He also, **however**, contends that it causes people and societies an unacceptable amount of suffering.

In both sentences, the transition serves exactly the same purpose: to connect the second statement to the first. Version 2 simply moves the transition to a less-expected location, drawing the reader's attention and emphasizing the contrast between the two statements.

One word of caution, though: don't get carried away. It is unnecessary to include a transition in every sentence, or even in every other sentence. These words and phrases should only be used to signal that you are genuinely taking a new "step" in your argument; using transitions for the sake of doing so will not improve the clarity of your writing.

Vary Your Sentences

Consider the following paragraph:

> John F. Kennedy successfully read his inaugural address to a large crowd of Americans as he took the oath of office on January 20th, 1961. Thousands of people were standing outside listening to JFK speak, as he explained that this new beginning would be considered a great change within the country. His clear and compelling speech led many people to approve of him and trust the changes he wanted to make for the country. Kennedy used anaphora as a way to emphasize his point to the audience.

There's nothing exactly wrong with the writing here: there are no grammatical errors, and the ideas are perfectly clear. Stylistically, though, it leaves something to be desired. It's perfectly fine to repeat the same sentence structure sometimes, but here it's excessive. Compare it to this version, which is much more varied and interesting to read.

> On January 20th, 1961, John F. Kennedy successfully read his inaugural address to a large crowd of Americans as he took the oath of office. Thousands of people were standing outside listening to JFK speak, as he explained that this new beginning would be considered a great change within the country. As a result of his clear and compelling speech, which relied on anaphora to make its point, many people began to approve of him and trust the changes he wanted to make for the country.

Punctuating Quotations

The Rhetorical Analysis Essay requires you to cite from the source documents provided, so you should be comfortable punctuating quotations. One of the trickier uses of quotation marks involves direct and indirect speech.

- In **direct speech**, a person's words are presented directly. Quotation marks are required.
- In **indirect speech**, the writer restates a person's words. No quotation marks are used.

Compare these two sentences from a hypothetical (imaginary) essay.

Direct: In his essay, Garrison denounces slavery as a sinful institution and asserts that the question of emancipation is not subject to debate. As Garrison proclaims, **"it admits no compromise."**

Indirect: Denouncing slavery as a sinful institution, Garrison proclaims that the question of emancipation is one **that does not allow for compromise.**

Notice that in the "indirect" version, no quotation marks are used because Garrison's words have been **rephrased** by the writer.

Incorrect: Denouncing slavery as a sinful institution, Garrison proclaims that the question of emancipation is one that **"does not allow for compromise."**

Notice also that no comma is placed after the word *that.*

Incorrect: Denouncing slavery as a sinful institution, Garrison proclaims that the question of emancipation is one **that, does** not allow for compromise.

Likewise, when a phrase such as *he claims* or *she states* does not immediately precede a direct quotation, **no comma should be used**. Quotation marks are still required, though.

Incorrect: Denouncing slavery as a sinful institution, Garrison proclaims that the question of **emancipation, "admits** no compromise."

Correct: Denouncing slavery as a sinful institution, Garrison proclaims that the question of **emancipation "admits** no compromise."

In addition, if you wish to condense a quotation, you must use **ellipses** (three dots) to show that material has been left out.

Correct: Garrison states, "I cannot but regard oppression in every form...with indignation."

And if you change a word or phrase in order to integrate a quotation into a sentence, the altered information should be placed in **brackets**.

Correct: Garrison states that "[he] cannot but regard oppression in every form—and most of all, that which turns a man into a thing—with indignation."

Diction

Diction simply means "word choice," and it applies to your own writing as much as the passage you are analyzing. One of the key differences between lower- and higher-scoring essays is the level of vocabulary they employ. Although it is unnecessary to flood your writing with "ten-dollar" words, sprinkling a handful of moderately sophisticated terms throughout your essays will help make them seem more polished and less casual.

For example, consider the following two paragraphs.

Version 1

People had two different views of slavery in the early 1800s. According to one view, the slaves should be freed gradually. The other view said that slaves should be freed right away because slavery went against basic human rights. This was far less popular. William Lloyd Garrison strongly refused to listen to the defenders of slavery and became an abolitionist instead.

Like some of the other "adequate" versions we've looked at, this paragraph is fine—it's just not stellar. While it gets its point across perfectly clearly, it does not include a particularly varied or challenging vocabulary.

Compare it to the second version, which strategically and naturally weaves in a handful of more sophisticated terms, without going overboard.

Version 2

Two views of slavery **dominated** American thinking in the early 1800s. One view **advocated** the gradual emancipation of slaves. The other view **promoted** immediate emancipation and was based upon the belief that slavery **violated** basic human rights. This view was far less popular. William Lloyd Garrison **staunchly** refused to listen to the **apologists** for slavery and became an **outspoken** abolitionist instead.

In contrast to Version 1, Version 2 is more polished and precise, not to mention more interesting to read.

Strong writing is also **specific**. While there are many ways to make your essays more specific, there are also a few common constructions to avoid.

1) "Hanging" pronouns

Although it is fine to use an occasional *this* or *that* without a noun afterward, you should not do so excessively. This construction can easily become vague and ambiguous, forcing your reader to work harder than necessary to figure out exactly what you are saying.

Vague: The problem with just stating complex points like **that**, unfortunately, is that people cannot just read **this** and understand the entire meaning of **that**.

In addition, statements beginning with *what* can easily become problematic.

Vague: Rosa Parks became a heroine of the Civil Rights movement because of **what she did**.

Instead of just referring to "what she did," you need to **explicitly state** what she did.

Specific: Rosa Parks became a heroine of the Civil Rights movement because **she refused to give up her seat and move to the back of the bus**.

2) "Vague" nouns

Although nouns are almost always more specific than pronouns, there are exceptions—most notably the word *thing(s)*. If possible, find an alternative.

Vague: In her speech to the Women's National Press Club, Clare Boothe Luce uses many **things**, including diction, repetition, and parallel structure, to prepare the members of the Press Club for her critique of their profession.

Specific: In her speech to the Women's National Press Club, Clare Boothe Luce uses many **devices**, including diction, repetition, and parallel structure, to prepare the members of the Press Club for her critique of their profession.

Passive Voice

In an **active** construction, the subject comes before the object:

Active:	William Shakespeare	wrote	*Hamlet*.
	subject	**verb**	**object**

In a passive construction, the subject and object are flipped:

Passive:	*Hamlet*	was written	by	William Shakespeare.
	subject	**verb**		**object**

Although the passive is commonly treated as something of a grammatical punching bag—some guides go so far as to offer what amounts to a blanket prohibition of it—there are times when it is perfectly appropriate for a given situation. For example, it may be used to emphasize that a person was on the receiving end of an action or, in the case of constructions involving *it*, to call attention to the impersonal nature of an action.

On the other hand, the repeated and indiscriminate use of the passive can create some very awkward constructions indeed. Unfortunately, that is exactly what tends to show up in students' essays.

Passive: In his speech, anaphora **is used by Kennedy** as a way to emphasize his point to the audience. **It is repeatedly explained by him** to the crowd of people listening that he does not want the country to be split into different groups, but that a major change **is required by the country**.

In the above example, the repeated use of passive constructions creates a general sense of awkwardness in the prose. Far from seeming more advanced or sophisticated, the writing is merely bogged down by all the unnecessary words.

Active: In his speech, **Kennedy uses anaphora** as a way to emphasize his point to the audience. **He repeatedly explains** to the crowd of people listening that he does not want the country to be split into different groups, but that **the country requires a major change**.

In this version, the active constructions make the writing cleaner, clearer, and easier for the reader to absorb.

In the next section, we're going to look at two examples of student essays. Because of copyright restriction, the text unfortunately cannot be reprinted here. It can, however, be found online at http://teachers.stjohns.k12.fl.us/vecchiola-m/files/2014/08/1996-Gary-Soto-Prompt.pdf. (Alternately, you can google "Gary Soto AP," and this link should appear at the top of the page.)

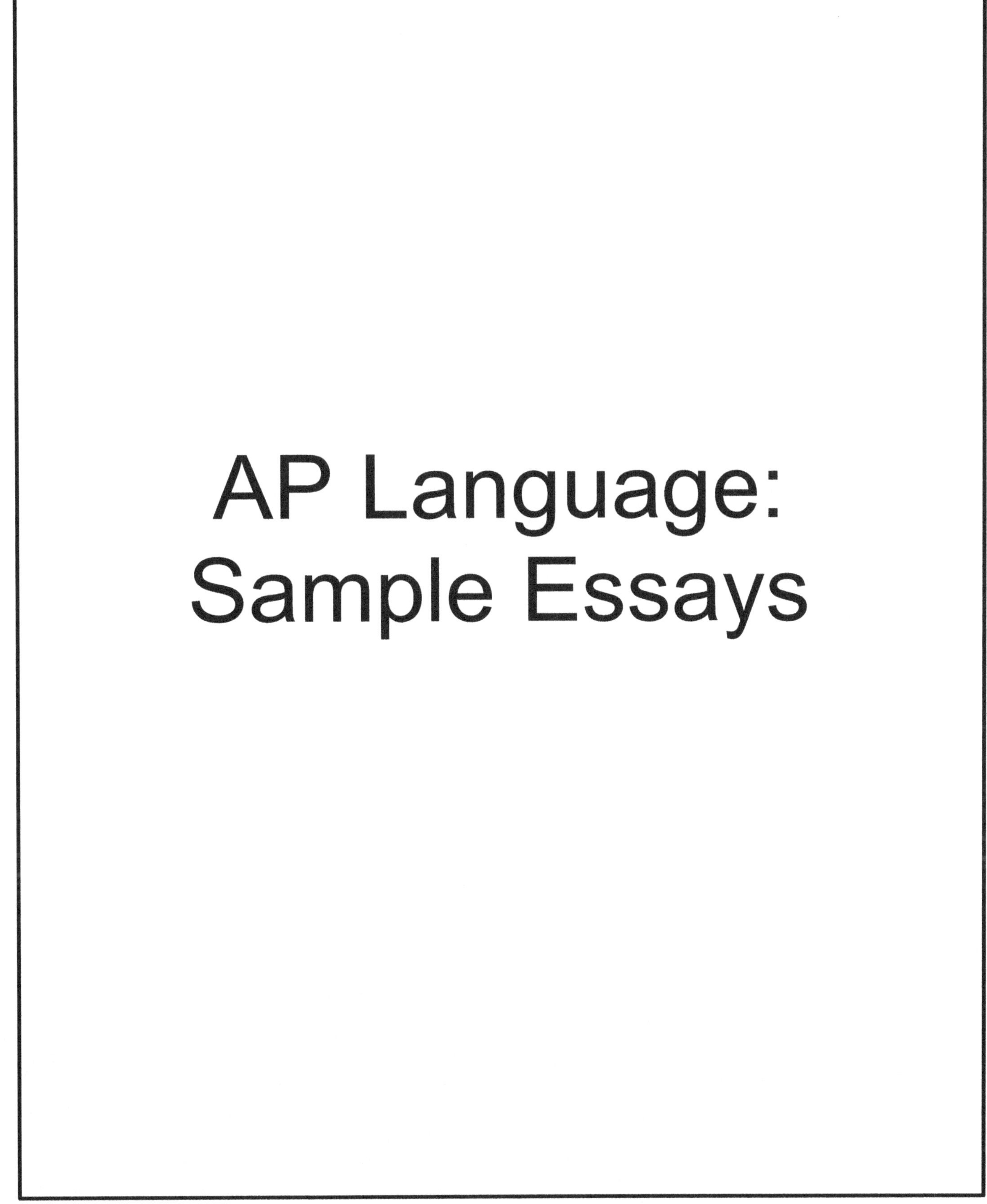

AP Language: Sample Essays

Note: Because of copyright restrictions, the passages on which the following essays are based cannot be reprinted here. They can be found online as follows:

Passage 1:

http://www.hamiltonunique.com/wp-content/uploads/2016/07/Gary-Soto.pdf

Passage 2:

https://securemedia.collegeboard.org/apc/_ap06_frq_englishlang_51616.pdf
(or google "plastic pink flamingo AP").

Sample Rhetorical Analysis Essay 1

Amidst the quick-paced lifestyles of modern society, one may often perceive that "time truly flies." This perspective becomes more apparent when one reflects upon the past. In the autobiographical narrative A Summer Life, Gary Soto presents a cogent description of his experience as a guilty, six-year-old. **By using vivid imagery, clever diction, repetition, and analogies, Soto illustrates that while sin can be enticing, facing truth and reality can be painful.**

The **first tool** Soto utilizes to draw the audience into his narrative is powerful imagery. In describing his sin, Soto equates the reward of apple pie to "sweet and gold-colored in the afternoon sun" (40). The statement that he "felt like crying because it was about the best thing [he] had ever tasted" (Soto 42-43) builds upon the imagery to underscore the idea that sin is akin to a sweet, mind-numbing substance. With these statements, Soto suggests that the immediate return one may acquire by sinning is dangerous and addictive. Similar to how Soto's childhood self realized that "the best things in life came stolen" (Soto 45-46), one may discover, after being introduced to an immoral act, for instance, that one actually enjoys engaging in the act. In this manner, one is only further attracted to the act and ultimately leads oneself to demise. This parallels Soto's narrative and introduces the idea that guilt might in fact be beneficial to the person it affects.

Soto **builds upon this idea** by using specific words in conjunction with repetition to emphasize that while the truth is painful, it can guide one back to the proper path. First, Soto scatters negatively connotated words such as "nailed," "forked," "clawing," and "glared" throughout his narrative (22, 23, 38, 63). These four words exhibit a mildly combative and violent nature. By associating such words with the events that follow his crime, Soto implies that although the pie gave him temporary joy, it ultimately left him with a potpourri of negative consequences. For example, Soto falsely perceived that "the driver knew," "Mrs. Hancock... knew," and "My mom... knew" he had stolen a pie (65, 66, 68). The mild fear that Soto experienced when he mistakenly thought in this way serves to emphasize that the consequences of sin are not necessarily worth the **fleeting** comfort sin provides. Additionally, the repetition of "knew" **illuminates** that the guilt one may experience after sinning is a vice with which one must **incessantly grapple**. Soto essentially suggests that one should avoid **indulging** in sinful behavior on a whim and should instead use one's desire for comfort, joy, entertainment, or other positive emotions as an incentive to discourage sin.

Lastly, Soto provides several impacts of the lesson he learned from his experience by incorporating religious analogies and allusions. Soto references God in addition to "flowery dust priests give off" and "the shadow of angels" several times in the narrative as a way to show that one should keep one's beliefs and values in mind before committing acts of evil or immorality (14-15). He further uses impactful statements such as "I knew sin was what you took and didn't give back" (Soto 85-86) to emphasize the importance of facing the painful truth— such statements in his narrative may be surprising to the reader, which then draws the reader's attention to the statements.

In "A Summer Life," Gary Soto effectively shows that one should not indulge in momentary measures but should instead focus on long-term consequences through the use of imagery, diction, repetition, analogies, and allusions. While time may pass quickly, Soto conveys that being true to oneself makes time pass in a much more pleasurable and memorable manner.

Score: 6/6 (Thesis: 1; Evidence and Commentary: 4; Sophistication: 1)

The piece effectively analyzes Soto's use of imagery, diction, and allusions to explain how the author conveys a sense of both guilt and pleasure resulting from a childhood sin. It is coherent and well-organized, and maintains a tight focus throughout, allowing the reader to follow each step of the writer's argument with ease. The analysis is extremely clear, permitting the reader to obtain a solid understanding of how the Soto text functions without even reading it.

Importantly, the introduction ends with a clear and specific thesis (*By using vivid imagery, clever diction, repetition, and analogies, Soto illustrates that while sin can be enticing, facing truth and reality can be painful*) that easily earns the writer 1 point. In addition to providing a specific focus for the essay, this statement also "previews" its structure, telling the reader precisely how the argument will, and does, develop.

In addition, rather than offer a brief and superficial discussion of numerous rhetorical strategies, each paragraph corresponds to exactly one rhetorical device (imagery, diction, allusions), which is then explicated thoroughly, with detailed and relevant examples. That earns the writer a maximum of 4 points in the "Evidence and Commentary" category.

The use of sophisticated terms such as *equates*, *demise*, *potpourri*, *fleeting*, *illuminates*, and *indulging* also gives an impression of advanced rhetorical control and earns the writer 1 point in "Sophistication." There are a few awkward turns of phrase, e.g., *negatively connotated words* rather than *words with negative connotations*, and *leads oneself to demise* rather than *leads to one's demise;* however, the essay is sufficiently strong as a whole that these lapses do not interfere in any significant way.

One thing you should be aware of: because this excerpt is taken from a memoir rather than a speech, it is not directed toward a specific audience, and the writer does not need to take the author/reader relationship into account. Although the essay itself was written recently, the source text was used on the 1996 (!) exam and may no longer reflect the types of texts used on the test. In addition to performing the type of analysis done in this essay, you also should be prepared to discuss the relationship between author and audience.

Sample Rhetorical Analysis Essay 2

The attraction to material culture is present throughout a multitude of ethnic groups and is a powerful force that can drive trends in society. This force manifests itself in the form of the pink flamingo, which rapidly gained popularity in the 1950's and became a prominent symbol of US popular culture. Author Jennifer Price takes on the task of analyzing the significance of this symbol in one of her written works. In "The Plastic Pink Flamingo: A Natural History," Price utilizes diverse examples and repetition of visual descriptions as she shifts from a description of the attractiveness of the flamingo in US culture to its presence in a variety of cultures across time periods to prove that US popular culture, which spreads as quickly as fire, tends to over-emphasize materialism and overlook negative trends in history while evidencing the fact that humans are often drawn to eccentric and eye-catching figures and innovations.

Price first employs a variety of examples to convince the reader that the flamingo, as a widely used symbol of uniqueness and specialty, reflects US society's predisposition to honor those with clearly visible indicators of high status and wealth. She introduces the widespread intrigue with the flamingo by describing its role in the lives of "Early Christians" (Price 54), in "ancient Egypt" (Price 55), and "In Mexico and the Caribbean" (Price 56-57) as a symbol of divinity and as a commonly used motif. In doing so, Price establishes that the flamingo's unique appearance (its pink color) has the power to draw a person's attention regardless of his or her ethnicity, upbringing, and background. She goes on to imply that Americans are no less susceptible to this behavior of being attracted to physical attributes by pointing out that "Americans had been flocking to Florida and returning home with flamingo souvenirs" (Price 4-5). Price elaborates upon the unnecessary emphasis placed upon superficial qualities as she associates the flamingo's pink color with "boldness" (Price 31). Citing Elvis Presley, who in his own time was rather bold and eccentric, as another follower of the pink flamingo trend due to his purchase of a "pink Cadillac" (44-45), Price essentially suggests that just as buying such a car was previously unthinkable, so was the emphasis placed upon pink flamingos in the 1950s. Furthermore, her inclusion of the fact that Presley purchased the car "right after he signed his first recording contract" (Price 43-44) implies that the favoring of the flamingos is impulsive, rash, and founded on temporary emotions.

Price expands upon this idea by using a multitude of strong adjectives to describe the flamingos. In using words such as "bright" (12), "flashy" (32), "broiling" (34), "sassy" (40), "hottest" (40), and "boldness" (31) to describe the flamingos' appearance, Price evidences the idea that humans are naturally drawn to eye-catching figures. While she does not explicitly state that such a trend is harmful, she does cite a historical example in which it was: "Americans had hunted flamingos to extinction in Florida in the late 1800s, for plumes and meat" (Price 13-15). With this piece of evidence, Price continues her line of thought to underscore that sometimes, submitting to a figure's attractiveness might not be worth the costs of doing so. She connects this idea to US culture at the time— while US culture boasted of the recent escape from the Depression, it proved to be a false sense of ecstasy and accomplishment to the American public. The flamingo essentially serves as a way to mask the deeper issues of the 1950's— it is a temporary solace for those who need a boost in morale. The flamingo's bright appearance and over-exaggerated colors mask its true nature as a simple plastic figurine. In a similar manner, the celebration of "new affluence" (Price 38-39) masks the residual issues that still affect the US. Price subtly characterizes the flamingo as a harmful distractor from real-world issues— the repetition of strong visual descriptions hints at the fact that preoccupation with superficial, more noticeable features ultimately distracts people and even entire nations from the hidden, but more pressing issues within society.

In her article, Price describes how US popular culture is able to spread like a fire throughout the country. At the same time, she cautions the reader that the brightness of such a fire has the power to eclipse the damage it might cause. Ultimately, by using multicultural examples and emphasizing visual descriptions, Price convinces the reader to keep this thought in mind and to be aware of the subtle, possibly harmful implications of trends in popular culture.

Score: 5/6 (Thesis: 1; Evidence and Commentary: 3; Sophistication: 1)

This is another successful essay, if not quite as strong and focused as the previous example.

Overall, the writer provides a cogent, detailed, and well-developed analysis of Price's essay, with a clear—if wordy—thesis (last sentence of the first paragraph). Note that the essay contains two rather than the traditional three body paragraphs: in this case, all the paragraphs are well developed, and so this less common organization does not prohibit the piece from receiving a high score. Each body paragraph develops a specific idea (the flamingo symbolizes the American tendency to worship high-status individuals; Price uses adjectives to emphasize that people's attraction to the flamingos was based on superficial emotions) and develops it with detailed examples. The conclusion effectively "opens up" the discussion beyond the flamingos to include a larger point about *subtle, possibly harmful implications of trends in popular culture.*

Aside from a few awkward phrasings (e.g., *specialty* as a synonym for *uniqueness*), the writer demonstrates strong technical and stylistic control. The essay includes a number of challenging words (*manifests, eccentric, rash, residual, underscore*) as well as complex punctuation and syntax, e.g., a colon and dashes in the third paragraph, and parallel structure with *just as…so* near the end of the second paragraph. These elements provide variety and lift the essay above run-of-the-mill high school writing, earning 1 point in "Sophistication."

That said, the writer does not always clearly establish how examples support claims. As key points, "diverse examples/a variety of examples" and "strong adjectives" are overly general. The writer does not say, for example, what specific types of adjectives Price uses (e.g., positive, negative, associated with a particular type of imagery).

In addition, while clear "markers" are provided at the beginning of each body paragraph to signal a new step in the argument (*Price first employs, Price expands on*), the second body paragraph feels more like an extension of the previous paragraph than like a separate point. The paragraphs themselves are also less tightly focused and precise than those in the earlier essay, and the reader must work just a little harder than necessary to follow the logic of the argument. As a result, only 3 points are earned for "Evidence and Commentary."

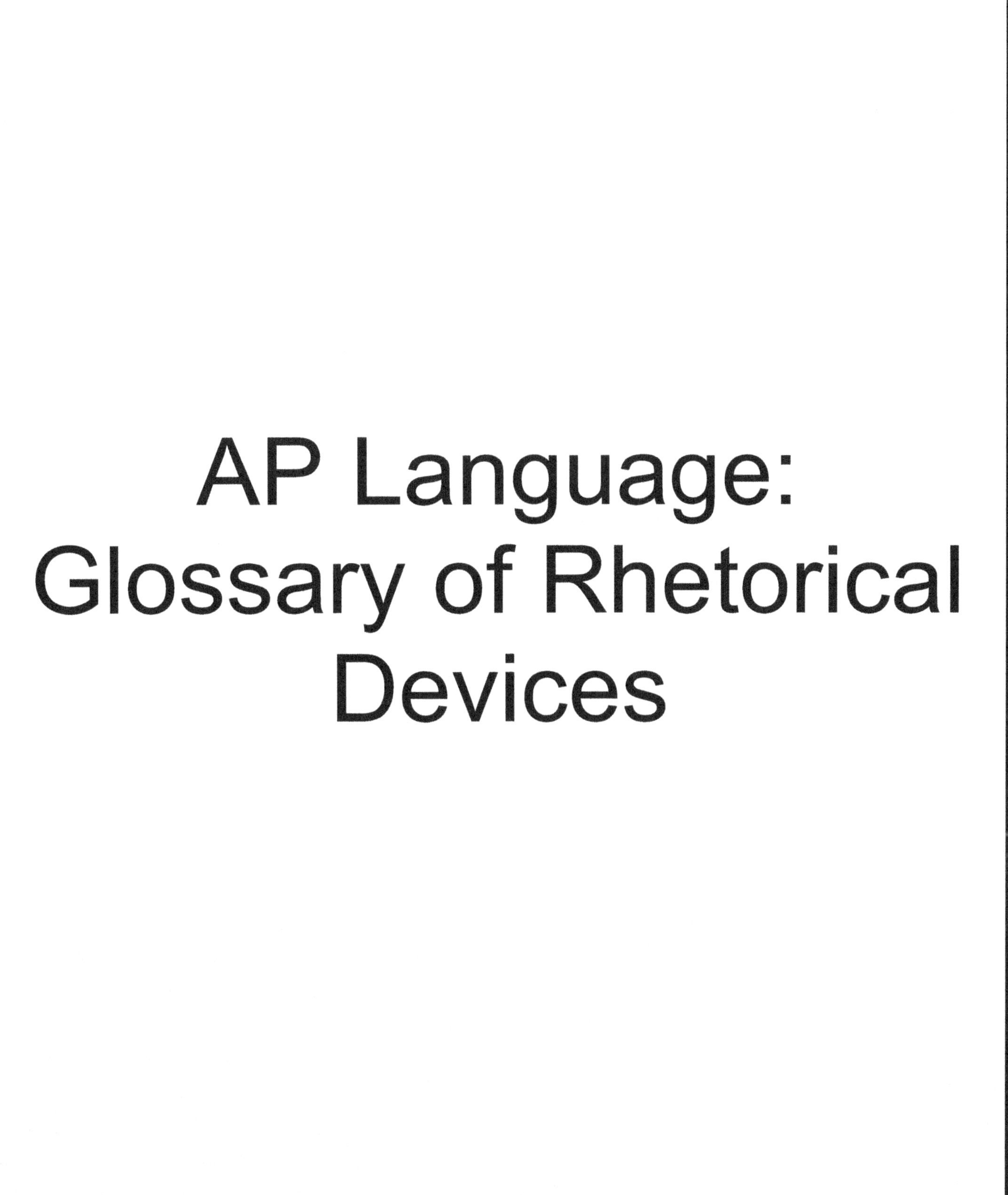

AP Language: Glossary of Rhetorical Devices

Glossary

Abstract Language – vague and generalized speech, full of references to intangible concepts.

Example: [S]ince **faith** itself cannot be proved by extraneous evidence, the safest course is to believe in the moral government of the world and therefore in the supremacy of the **moral law**, the law of **truth** and **love**. Exercise of faiths will be the safest where there is the clear determination summarily to reject **all** that is contrary to **truth** and **love**.

Accusation – Charge of guilt or wrongdoing.

Acknowledgment – Recognition of the validity of an (opposing) idea.

Counterargument – Example or idea that supports an opposing argument, or that weakens an author's argument.

Concession – Acknowledgment that an opposing view or argument is valid, or that part of one's argument has a weakness.

See p. 18 for a discussion of these terms.

Allegory – An allegory is a story in which the main elements (characters, settings, etc.) all function as symbols for something else. Although an allegory may be discussed or referred to in a passage, passages themselves are normally too short and concrete to serve as full-length allegories.

Alliteration – Repetition of the same sound at the beginnings of multiple words.

Example: I favor, as a **p**ractical **p**olicy, the **p**utting of first things first.

Allusion – Reference, usually to a work of art, literature, or well-known story or place.

Example: The United States recently crossed a digital **Rubicon**: for the first time, more data was sent over wireless devices than by telephone.

The Rubicon is a river in Italy, and the phrase *crossing the Rubicon* means "passing a point of no return" because Julius Caesar crossed it with his army in 49 A.D. and began a civil war.

Anachronism – A person/object that is out of place in its time period and belongs to a different era.

Analogy – Comparison, typically in the form "x is to y" but also in the form of either a simile or a metaphor; used to make a point about someone or something.

Example: [Zora Neale Hurston] was not a joiner of movements or trends. **Like her hometown, Hurston was iconoclastic**.

An **Extended Analogy** is an analogy that continues beyond a single comparison, lasting for several sentences or even a paragraph.

Example: The dance **revolution** was fought on many fronts, but the **key battle** took place at Vermont's Bennington College. It was here in the 1930s, amid the cow farms in the bucolic Green Mountains, that the giants of modern dance—Graham, Humphrey, Holm, Weidman—fine-tuned their techniques and trained their **dancer armies** to **spread the revolution** across the country.

Anaphora - Repetition of a word or phrase at the beginning of a series of consecutive sentences/statements.

Example: **We shall** not flag or fail. **We shall** go on to the end. **We shall** fight in France, **we shall** fight on the seas and oceans, **we shall** fight with growing confidence and growing strength in the air, **we shall** defend our island, whatever the cost may be...

(Personal) Anecdote - A brief story. A **personal anecdote** is simply a story told from an author or narrator's perspective.

Shortcut: I, my, me

Example: On a mid-August day with a heat index of 115 degrees, in a rental car with slow pickup, **I** drive through the Orlando suburbs searching for Eatonville, a three-square-mile town of 2,400 residents. **I** keep getting lost. Finally a brown "Eatonville Historic District" sign appears, and fifteen miles later it dawns on **me** that **I** have gone too far. I turn back, find the city limits, and enter Eatonville. At the "Welcome to Maitland" sign, **I** realize **I** have driven through the entire town. It took three minutes.

Antithesis - Use of parallel structure to set opposing ideas in contrast to one another.

Example: Winter and summer, then, were two hostile lives, and bred two separate natures. **Winter was always the <u>effort to live</u>; summer was <u>tropical license</u>**.

Appeal to Emotion (Pathos) - Use of strong or highly charged language to elicit an emotional response.

Example: The eye of the reformer is met with **angry** flashes, portending **disastrous** times; but his heart may well **beat lighter** at the thought that America is young, and that she is still in the impressible stage of her existence. May he not hope that **high lessons** of **wisdom, of justice and of truth**, will yet give direction to her destiny? Were the nation older, the patriot's heart might be **sadder**, and the reformer's brow **heavier**. Its future might be **shrouded in gloom**, and the hope of its prophets **go out in sorrow**.

Appeal to Ethics or Authority (Ethos) – Establishment of credibility on moral grounds, or by citing authorities in a field.

Example: [W]e have an obligation to our **common prosperity** and our **common humanity** to extend a hand to those emerging markets and impoverished people who are suffering the most.

Appeal to Reason (Logos) – Use of logical arguments, including facts and statistics.

Example: In the United States we have a **capitalistic economy**. That is because public opinion favors that type of economy under the conditions in which we live. But we have imposed certain restraints; for instance, we have **antitrust laws**. These are the **legal evidence** of the determination of the American people to maintain an economy of free competition and not to allow monopolies to take away the people's freedom.

Aside – Parenthetical remark used to offer commentary or address the reader directly.

Shortcut: Parentheses

Example: In an era when few men and no women received such international renown, Dolley Madison's stature has perplexed historians and modern Americans **(who associate her name with ice cream and a line of packaged pastries)**.

Assertion – Declarative statement or claim.

Statements of assertion are usually topic sentences and/or located at key places within an argument (e.g., the last sentence of the first paragraph). Assertions are typically blunt and are characterized by a tone of great confidence; they do not include support or explanations.

Example: **Ideas matter.** A relatively small number can be classed as major historical events. And many times, their best, most eloquent expression has been on paper, stamped in ink, sewn on one side, and bound between hard covers.

Assonance – Repetition of a vowel sound within a group of words.

Example: The sp**i**der skins **lie** on their s**i**des, translucent and ragged, their legs dr**y**ing in knots.

Cliché – Trite saying that expresses a common or banal idea.

Examples:

- A bird in the hand is worth two in the bush.
- What goes around comes around.
- As light as a feather.
- Every cloud has a silver lining.

Comparison – Discussion of the similarities between two people or things.

Shortcut: **Like, similar to, just as**

Example: **Just like** human beings, chimpanzees can share a joke but they are also capable of sharing laughter even when they don't find something particularly funny. A recent study of wild chimpanzees has found that laughter occurs not just when chimps are enjoying themselves but also when they want to promote social bonding—**much like** human smiles help people relate to one another in a conversation.

Contrast – Discussion of the differences between two people or two things.

Shortcut: **Unlike, in contrast to**

Example: The **essential difference** between literary and scientific style is the use of metaphor. What counts in science is the importance of the discovery. Lyrical expression in literature, **on the other hand,** is a device to communicate emotional feeling directly from the mind of the writer to the mind of the reader.

Comparisons may include either literal (as in the above example) or **figurative language**. Types of comparisons that use figurative language include **similes, metaphors,** and **personification** (described later in this section).

(Detailed) Description – (Vivid) account or recollection of a person, object, event, etc.

Shortcut: Lots of modifiers (adjectives and adverbs) and imagery

Example: There's a picture of Hines with his band on the stage at the Pearl Theater in Philadelphia, **exuding swank**. Their suit pants, which bear **stripes of black satin** down the seams, break **perfectly** over their **gleaming** shoes; their jacket lapels have the **span of a Madagascar fruit bat**; their hair is slicked. They were on top of their world.

Digression – Off-topic discussion. Note that most passages are too short/focused to contain digressions.

Direct Citation/Quotation – word-for-word transcription of words spoken or written by someone other than the author.

Shortcut: Quotation marks

Example: Make no mistake—Dolley Madison was as fiercely partisan as any male politician. Her declaration, **"I confess I do not admire contention in any form, either political or civil"** is often cited by historians as proof of her pacific nature. The second half of the statement reveals more: **"I would rather fight with my hands than my tongue**..."

Dry/Wry Humor – Form of subtle, often dark, humor, frequently based on wordplay, irony, or sarcasm.

Example: The beginnings of planet building pose a remarkably intractable problem, to the point that one of the world's experts on the subject, Scott Tremaine, has elucidated (partly in **jest**) Tremaine's laws of planet formation. **The first of these laws states that "all theoretical predictions about the properties of exosolar planets are wrong," and the second that "the most secure prediction about planet formation is that it can't happen."** Tremaine's **humor** underscores the ineluctable fact that planets do exist, despite our inability to explain this astronomical enigma.

Although the words *jest* (kidding) and *humor* indirectly indicate that Tremaine's "laws" are supposed to be funny, you need to think about what they're actually saying in order to understand the humor. Tremaine is making fun of the difficulty scientists have in understanding the beginning of the universe by using typically dry, scientific language to state complete absurdities. It is of course ridiculous to suggest that *the most secure prediction about planet formation is that it can't happen* because if that were true, there would be no Earth and no people. Tremaine himself wouldn't exist, and he certainly couldn't have written this passage!

Euphemism – Replacement of an offensive or unpleasant word with a less offensive one.

Example: The early years of the telephone brought concerns over the unwanted entry—via telephone line—of **unsavory characters** into the home, and some people called for laws to regulate criminal use of the phone.

Here, the more refined phrase *unsavory characters* replaces the much blunter *criminals*.

Exclamation – A brief, forceful outcry or utterance.

Shortcut: Exclamation point

Example: ...Then he cried loudly, his face turned toward the door, causing the walls of the room to echo: **"They are approaching!"**

Flashback – Insertion of an earlier event into a narrative, jumping back in time.

Generalization – Broad statement or assertion.

Example: Studies show that when **we** read nonfiction, **we** read with our shields up. **We** are critical and skeptical. But when **we** are absorbed in a story, **we** drop our intellectual guard. **We** are moved emotionally, and this seems to make **us** rubbery and easy to shape. But perhaps the most impressive finding is just how fiction shapes **us**. Fiction enhances **our** ability to understand other people; it promotes a deep morality.

Hyperbole (Exaggeration) – Overstated or over-the-top language employed for dramatic or humorous effect.

Example: [Edmund Wilson] was the Nureyev at what he did—a genius, really: probably **the greatest reader America has ever known**.

Hypothesis/Speculation – Prediction of an outcome.

Example: Why did nineteenth-century American women feel obliged to wear thin slippers at all times and in all seasons when English women apparently felt free to match their shoes to their circumstances? It **may be** that the very fluidity of American class structure increased the pressure on women to be dependent and ladylike.

Irony – Incongruity (gap) between what would logically be expected from a situation and what actually occurs.

Example: Hurricanes—some of the **largest, most fearful** storms produced by the Earth system—are <u>blown around</u> the planet by **much weaker** storms.

Metaphor – Comparison that does not state that *x is like/as y*, but rather than *x* <u>*is*</u> *y*.

Example: The dance **revolution** was fought on many fronts, but the **key battle** took place at Vermont's Bennington College.

Metonymy – Replacement of a literal word or phrase by a closely related one.

Example: Not fewer than forty Americans have, within the past two years, been hunted down and, without a moment's warning, hurried away in chains, and consigned to slavery and excruciating torture. Some of these have had wives and children, dependent on them for **bread**.

In the above example, *bread* is used as a substitute for food in general.

Oratory – Dramatic and rousing speech.

Oxymoron – Two contradictory terms placed next to one another for contrast.

Examples:

- deafening silence
- jumbo shrimp
- painfully sweet

Paradox – Statement or situation that appears illogical or contradictory but that may reveal an underlying truth.

Example: The case of Henry Thoreau stands as proof for the whole notion of human inscrutability. **This man told us more of himself than perhaps any other American writer, and still he remains beyond fathoming**.

Parallel Structure – Repetition of the same word or group of words at the same place (usually the beginning) in consecutive sentences. Parallel structure can also be a form of repetition.

Example: As we are asked to contemplate the disappearance of books as such, it's worth pausing over the astonishing range of…purposes that have been served by books: **the** liberation **of** individuals, **the** reinforcement **of** community, **the** propagation **of** orthodoxy, **the** expansion **of** self-knowledge, **the** publication **of** scientific findings, education and delectation, insult and calumny, **the** spread **of** lies and promulgation of facts, public good and private satisfaction.

Paraphrase – Shortened restatement of a passage or text, usually for clarification.

Shortcut: That is (to say), In other words

Passive Voice – Construction in which the subject and object of a sentence are flipped in order to emphasize that someone or something was on the receiving end of an action. Instead of x did y, a passive construction emphasizes that y was done by x. This strategy is typically used either to make writing more objective or less personal, or to deflect responsibility away from an individual.

Example: During his presidency, James Madison **was hampered by what Dolley called "a Capricious Senate,"** whose objections she characterized as "almost treason."

In the above sentence, the passive voice emphasizes that Madison was the object of the Senate's actions, implying that his inability to govern effectively was not his own fault.

Personification – Attribution of human characteristics to an inanimate object.

Example: **Five-fingered** ferns hung over the water and **dropped** spray from their **fingertips**… The high mountain wind coasted, **sighing** through the pass and **whistled** on the edges of the big blocks of broken granite.

Qualification – Inclusion of additional information to soften a blunt or harsh statement, or to provide a more detailed understanding of a generalization.

Shortcut: dashes, parentheses

Example: **[General Statement]** There is nothing so stimulating for the hands and the mind as studying a musical instrument. **[Qualification]** The journey to mastery demands focus, discipline, lightness of touch, musical intuition, and persistence.

In the above example, the general statement is quite extreme: it states that *nothing* is as stimulating for the hands and the mind as studying an instrument. The second statement qualifies it by providing an explanation and giving examples of the various ways in which it stimulates the mind and the hands.

Repetition – Use of the same word or phrase multiple times within a given piece of text.

Example: **We** were the **people** with the noisy dog, the **people** who raised chickens. **We** were the foreigners on the block.

Rhetorical Question – Question asked without expectation of response, usually for dramatic effect or to emphasize a point.

Shortcut: Question marks

Example: Why did the residents of Washington City, the members of government and their families, and, indeed, all of America declare Dolley the nation's "Queen"? What did they understand about Dolley Madison that we don't?

Simile – Comparison using *like* or *as*.

Example: Named after the Greek Island of Lefkada, artist and author Lafcadio Hearn was **like** an island unto himself.

Synecdoche – Use of the part to represent the whole.

Example: It is pleasant to celebrate in this peaceful way, upon this **old mother soil**, the anniversary of an experiment which was born of war with this same land so long ago, and wrought out to a successful issue by the devotion of our ancestors. It has taken nearly a hundred years to bring the English and Americans into kindly and mutually appreciative relations, but I believe it has been accomplished at last.

In the above example, *soil* is used to represent the country of England as a whole.

Treatise – Formal, systematic work of writing about a subject.

Tribute – Testimonial praising a person's accomplishments or positive qualities.

Example: In his lifetime, Ronald Reagan was such a cheerful and invigorating presence that it was easy to forget what daunting historic tasks he set himself. He sought to mend America's wounded spirit, to restore the strength of the free world, and to free the slaves of communism.

Understatement (Litotes) – Use of excessively restrained language.

This is a form of irony and dry/wry humor, often used to satirize or mock.

Example: William Shakespeare is an author who has become **rather well known** for his theatrical writing.

Because Shakespeare is probably the best-known English dramatist in history, saying that he is *rather well known* constitutes a massive understatement.

Wordplay - Verbal wit or punning, often involving double meanings of words.

Example: Food is at the center of our anxieties about science and modernity, yet the truth is that it has become a scapegoat, or perhaps I should say *scapetofu,* for a host of imaginary sins we associate with technology.

A scape**goat** is an innocent person who gets blamed for someone else's wrongdoing. Here, the author is saying that people blame food for problems they wrongly believe technology has created.

By altering the original word and replacing *goat* (a type of meat) with *tofu* (a meat substitute that vegetarians are often made fun of for eating), the author is implicitly mocking people who subscribe to this belief.

In addition, the phrase *or should I say…* is deliberately coy and understated, the literary equivalent of a wink. His tone could thus be described as wry, or facetious, or ironic.

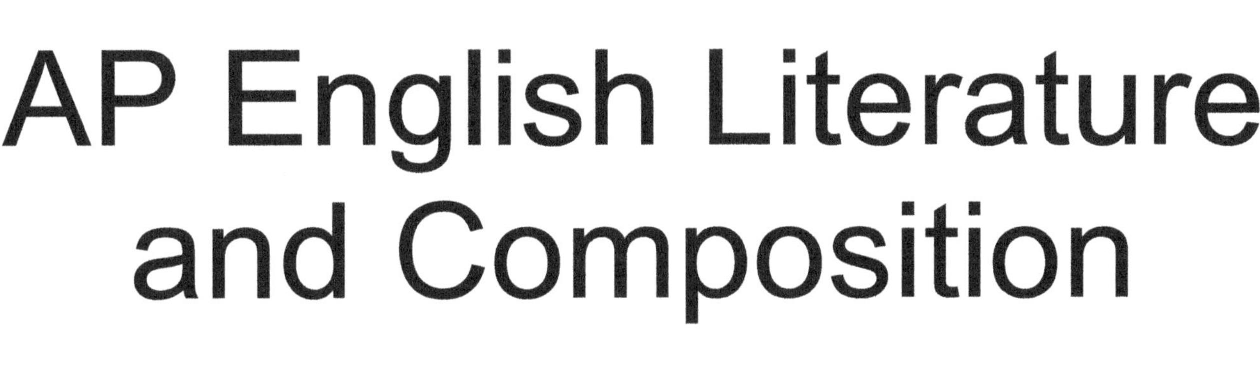

AP English Literature and Composition

The Prose Analysis Essay

The 2020 AP® English Literature and Composition Exam consists exclusively of the 45-minute Prose Analysis Essay (always Question #2 on the full-length exam).

You will be provided with a passage of around 65-85 lines from a contemporary or classic novel originally written in English and asked to craft a thesis-driven essay analyzing a particular aspect of the text and supporting it with specific details.

Although the passage is frequently drawn from an eighteenth- or nineteenth-century work and is generally quite challenging, the assignment does offer one major advantage: all the information you need is provided right in front of you, so there is no need to spend time thinking of outside examples.

Essays are scored by trained readers (primarily high school English teachers and college English professors). **The rubric awards points in three main categories, with possible scores ranging from 0 (lowest) to 6 (highest).**

Thesis: 0-1 point

This is the most straightforward and objective of the three main criteria: having a clear thesis earns you one point; not having a clear thesis gets you no points.

Note, however, that it is almost impossible to earn a zero on the essay while obtaining the maximum number of points in the other categories—by definition, an essay that lacks a clear thesis will be very difficult to support or argue in a sophisticated way.

- **1** - There is a clear, defensible thesis that takes a **specific position** on the prompt.
- **0** - The thesis is either absent, restates/rewords the prompt without taking a specific position, or extremely vague (e.g., it states that there are pros/cons to both sides of the argument but does not indicate which side the writer agrees with).

The thesis can appear anywhere in your essay—it does not need to be placed at the end of the first paragraph in order to earn the point. **In most cases, however, placing it in the introduction will help to keep your essay focused and on-topic.**

The thesis may also consist of more than one sentence, provided that the sentences are placed near each other and convey a coherent argument.

Evidence and Commentary: 0-4 points

These points are awarded based on how effectively you support your argument, and on the depth of your analyses and explanations.

4 - Essays that earn a top score provide specific evidence or explanations for each claim; they also make clear how evidence/explanations support the various claims so that the reader is able to follow the logic of the argument. They also explain how specific words and phrases support your argument. **Note that essays with serious grammatical errors cannot earn a 4.**

3 - Essays that earn a 3 demonstrate many of the same qualities as "4" essays but do not provide specific evidence or explanations for all claims and/or do not make (fully) clear how evidence supports arguments or claims.

2 - Essays that earn a 2 fail to provide specific evidence or explain reasoning inconsistently. They may also include information that is off-topic or does not support claims.

1 - Essays that earn a 1 make general claims rather than provide specific evidence and summarize evidence rather than explaining how it supports a claim.

0 - Essays that earn a 0 restate the thesis/information from the sources, or are off-topic.

Sophistication: 0-1 point

This is the most "open" of the three categories, and there are multiple ways to earn the point.

1 - This point can be earned for either the strength of the writing (e.g., precise and colorful vocabulary, varied sentence structure and punctuation, clear transitions) or the analyses (providing broader context for an argument, acknowledging counterarguments, discussing limitations of an argument).

0 - Essays that earn a 0 in this category contain none of the features necessary for a 1.

The point for sophistication is awarded based on an overall impression of engagement with the prompt and is thus more difficult to achieve than the "thesis" point.

If you are concerned about essay scoring, keep in mind that the readers do take effort into account and are encouraged to give you the benefit of the doubt. They are not looking for excuses to mark you down but rather want you to do well. Moreover, they are explicitly instructed to take into account that the essays are first drafts written under intense time pressure, and to assess them accordingly.

Although you may be most comfortable with the five-paragraph format, this structure is not required; it is, however, usually the most straightforward option. That said, if you believe that an alternate format is better suited to your argument, you are certainly free to use it.

Note: As of the end of April, the College Board has not indicated how scores will be translated from the 6-point essay rubric to the 5-point overall scale. As a result, you should simply focus on writing the strongest essay possible under the given circumstances.

What Exactly Is a Prose Analysis Essay?

As an AP Literature student, you are probably accustomed to writing literary analysis essays for English class. However, if your class hasn't done much preparation for the AP exam, or if you're self-studying for the AP test, you might not be quite sure how to approach this particular essay, or how it differs from the sorts of assignments you've received in school.

Essentially, the Prose Analysis Essay differs from a typical English paper in the sense that it requires you to focus on the "micro" aspect of a text. Rather than consider a particular aspect of a narrative or character across a full-length novel, you must instead focus on how these elements are depicted in only about 65-85 lines. Because you will almost certainly have never seen the passage before, or be familiar with the novel from which it is excerpted—passages tend to be taken from lesser-known works that are rarely studied in English classes—you will not be able to bring in outside knowledge about the work (novel or short story).

Although the question will impose some limits on your analysis, it will be sufficiently broad to allow you a good deal of leeway to focus on the aspects of the passage you find most interesting. Essentially, your goal is to act as a "tour guide" to the text—to indicate points of particular significance and explain how the author uses language to create specific effects or convey particular information about a character, event, or relationship. You should not feel obligated to cover the entire passage; rather, you should selectively focus on a few key places and discuss their importance to the passage as a whole.

While the AP Literature course description now emphasizes skills over knowledge, the reality is that it is very difficult to write a strong literary analysis without a reasonable knowledge of rhetorical devices; indeed, rhetoric *is* the language of literary analysis. For this reason, I have included an extended glossary of rhetorical figures at the end of this guide. It is certainly possible to score well on the Prose Analysis Essay with a discussion of only basic rhetorical techniques; however, the more tools you have in your toolbox, so to speak, the easier it will be for you to identify places of interest in the passage and analyze them effectively. **As much as possible, the specific features of the text should drive your thesis; formulating an argument based on a general impression and then going back and trying to find evidence to support it typically results in a much weaker analysis.** And given that you have only 45 minutes to analyze the passage and write your essay, the faster you can comfortably work, the less stressful the exam will be.

Two general points to keep in mind:

1) Score Correlates with Length

Generally speaking, longer essays tend to receive higher scores. More writing = more in-depth analysis. That said, **correlation is not causation**: An essay that is poorly structured, repetitive, and vague will not receive a high score, regardless of how long it is.

2) Aim for Clarity and Coherence, Not Brilliance

Your readers will understand that you wrote your essay about an unfamiliar text, under extreme time pressure. As a result, they do not expect your writing to be spectacularly brilliant. Rather, they are looking to see whether you can cobble together a coherent, well-supported argument that demonstrates a moderately insightful interpretation of the passage. Focus on conveying your thoughts clearly, not weighing them down with flowery language.

How to Write Your Thesis

Writing a strong thesis is a skill that many students find challenging, both on the AP Literature exam and in general. The "Thesis" point is, however, the most straightforward aspect of the rubric to master; it is also the central idea around which your entire essay will revolve. Without a clear thesis, it is extremely difficult—if not impossible—to develop your argument effectively and obtain full points in the other categories.

Simply put, **a thesis is an argument**, i.e., the main point: the central claim or assertion that your essay will be devoted to supporting.

To determine your thesis, you can use the following formula: **who + so what + how?**

In other words:

- Who is the passage about?
- What does the author convey about them?
- How does the author go about conveying it?

To be effective, a thesis must be both **specific** and **debatable**.

It is **NOT** a factual statement or a description of the plot/theme(s).

- Nathaniel Hawthorne was one of the most important American writers of the nineteenth century.
- The passage describes how the governess sees ghosts that no one else can see.
- The passage from a novel by Kate Chopin deals with women's role in society.

It should **NOT** stretch beyond the **scope** of the passage—that is, it should not be too general.

Prose passages consist of no more than around 100-110 lines and generally focus on no more than one or two characters (although additional characters may also be referred to).

Because of this narrow focus, your thesis should not consist of a grand, sweeping generalization about society or human nature.

- The passage reveals the universal human tendency to be manipulated by flattery.
- Throughout history, people have always attempted to achieve a higher social status.
- Some individuals will always feel compelled to rebel against society's conventions.

This type of overly broad language can easily make your essay seem unfocused and cost you the "Sophistication" point as well as the "Thesis" point. And because it is very difficult to support such an overly broad statement effectively, you will almost certainly lose points in the "Evidence and Commentary" category as well.

Theses that are less sweeping but still overgeneralized should also be avoided, as should theses that consist of too many parts. **If you make two claims in your thesis, for example, you will be expected to support <u>both</u> claims and will be penalized for not doing so.**

Although you may be awarded a point for the kinds of statements that appear below, they are difficult to develop in a focused way.

- The author shows how the characters have both similarities and differences.

- The author uses several techniques to reveal certain things about the characters.

- The author uses dialogue and diction to show that as members of society, people must take others' needs into consideration, and also to warn of the dangers of relying excessively on the approval of others.

In a literary analysis essay, **a strong thesis SHOULD address the specific literary techniques or devices** that the author uses to create a particular impression or convey an idea.

In addition to giving your essay clear focus, this information can also provide the essential structure of your essay—each main section (typically a paragraph, but more if necessary) can correspond to a particular technique.

In the examples below, notice how each of the "effective" options below provides a clear and precise argument that limits the scope of the discussion. While the specifics vary, these examples are based on the essential formula ***the author uses x to convey y.***

Ineffective: The passage from Kate Chopin's short story "The Storm" contains a lot of imagery and symbolism.

Effective: In the passage from the short story "The Storm," Kate Chopin uses short, choppy sentences and images of violent weather to symbolize the protagonist's rebellion against her conventional female role.

Ineffective: In the passage from Henry James' *The Turn of the Screw*, the governess clearly suffers from delusions.

Effective: In the passage from Henry James' *The Turn of the Screw*, the author employs rhetorical questions and fragmented statements to indicate the governess's increasingly delusional state.

Ineffective In the excerpt provided, Howells conveys the reality of war.

Effective: In the excerpt provided, Howells uses a combination of metaphor, irony, and pathos to create an almost grotesque parody of the reality of war.

Quick Check: Does It Get the Point?

Decide whether each of the statements below would receive the "Thesis" point. (Answers are at the end of the guide, on p. 110.)

1. Throughout the excerpt provided, the author uses literature to expose the truth while also being creative.

1 _________ 0 _________

2. The passage from Amy Tan's *The Joy Luck Club* has many descriptions of how Waverly Jong is both similar and different from her mother, Lindo.

1 _________ 0 _________

3. In the passage from the short story "The Birthmark," Hawthorne articulates the obsession with perfection through symbols, characters, and narrative voice.

1 _________ 0 _________

4. The passage from Edith Wharton's *The Age of Innocence* shows how Newland Archer and Countess Ellen Olenska behave among the many societal rules and double standards of the nineteenth century.

1 _________ 0 _________

5. In the excerpt from the short story "Bartleby the Scrivener," Melville utilizes contrasting series of long and short words, as well as a vocabulary of illness and destruction, to convey the narrator's tortured relationship to Bartleby.

1 _________ 0 _________

What to Look for in a Passage

Unlike the non-fiction passages that appear on the SAT, ACT, and AP English Language and Composition Exam, fiction passages do not contain arguments, nor are they intended to persuade readers or inspire them to take a particular action. Instead, Prose Analysis passages are chosen because they illustrate particular character traits and/or relationships between characters. Note that they may also be chosen because they are *not* entirely straightforward—that is, they may be open to multiple interpretations. As a result, there is no single "correct" answer, only responses that are more and less supported by the text.

You should therefore plan to read the passage with one central goal in mind: identify a major idea or character attribute that the author conveys, and note the specific places in the text where it is emphasized. In general, **key information is typically presented at the beginning and (re)emphasized at the end**, so you should make sure to pay particular attention to the first and last paragraphs. In addition, **make sure to read the blurb before the passage**—it may offer information necessary to keeping track of the characters or understanding the action.

The most effective way to approach this type of analysis is to have a list of specific textual features to look out for as you read. Although the assignment may suggest that you look for "style, tone, and selection of detail," responses that address only these elements in a general way are unlikely to achieve a high score in either the "Commentary and Evidence" or "Sophistication" category.

5 Key Questions:

1) Is the prevailing mood of the passage positive or negative? Why, and how do you know?

2) Does the passage contain any clear stylistic changes or shifts in focus? If so, where?

3) Is there any repetition of words/phrases? If so, what idea or trait does it emphasize?

4) Is there any "interesting" punctuation, e.g., question marks, dashes, or italics?

5) Diction: every passage contains diction, i.e., words. As a result, you should avoid merely stating that the author uses "diction." Rather, you should explain what **type of diction** is used. In particular, there are two simple things to consider:

   - Does the author use extreme language, e.g., *always, never, exceedingly, everywhere*, or vocabulary that is strongly positive or negative?

   - Does the author use language associated with a specific field, e.g., economics, medicine, war?

If you keep these questions in mind and mark down places of particular stylistic interest as you read, you will essentially have both your thesis and your primary points set right from the start.

Note that if you want to consider more complex literary devices, the glossary at the end of this guide provides a detailed list.

Tone and Attitude

Some Prose Analysis questions may explicitly direct you to focus on the narrator's attitude, but even if this aspect of the text is not mentioned, both tone and attitude are often key to understanding what the author wants to convey about a character or event.

Tone and attitude are similar concepts—at the most basic level, both indicate a positive, negative, or neutral stance—but they are not precisely the same thing. Essentially, tone involves specific features of the text, whereas attitude involves emotions.

In some cases, tone and attitude are clearly aligned: the author will use extremely positive or negative words (i.e., tone) to indicate a strongly (dis)approving attitude on the part of the narrator or a character. In the two excerpts below, for instance, the tone and the attitude are strongly correlated.

Positive: The young woman was tall, with a figure of **perfect elegance** on a large scale. She had dark and abundant hair, **so glossy that it threw off the sunshine with a gleam**; and a face which, besides being **beautiful** from **regularity** of feature and **richness** of complexion, had the **impressiveness** belonging to a marked brow and deep black eyes. She was ladylike, too…characterised by a certain **state and dignity**…

Negative: [H]is passion had less **terror** for her than his **coldness**. The increasing frequency of the latter mood told her the **sad news** that he **disliked** her with a **growing dislike**. The more interesting that her appearance and manners became under the softening influences which she could now command, and in her wisdom did command, the more she seemed to **estrange** him.

On the other hand, an author can also convey a distinctly approving or disapproving view by using a much more **moderate** tone—that is, by using less extreme language. In such cases, you must be able to pick up on the necessary cues to understand what the author is implying; indeed, **places in the text where there is a gap between tone and attitude are particularly strong candidates for analysis because of what they indirectly reveal.**

For example, consider this example from Louise Erdrich's novel *The Round House.*

Positive: Whenever I **succeeded** in working loose a tiny tree, I placed it like a **trophy** beside me on the narrow sidewalk that surrounded the house…I thought it was a **wonder** the treelets had **persisted** through a North Dakota winter.

In the above excerpt, the text is devoid of the kind of strong language that characterizes the earlier example, but the narrator nevertheless conveys a distinctly positive attitude through the use of words such as *succeeded, trophy, wonder,* and *persisted.* The description conveys a small-scale triumph of life over the harshness of nature, and the narrator's appreciation of that fact. In this case, the narrator happens to be a 13-year-old boy, and so this type of description suggests that he is unusually mature and perceptive for his age.

Compare it to this example from Howells' "Editha," which operates at a similar level of tone, but in the opposite direction.

Negative: [Editha] ran **impatiently** out on the veranda, to the edge of the steps, and **imperatively demanded greater haste of him with her will** before she called aloud to him: "George!"

Although the sentence is distinctly negative, Howells does not use over-the-top language to convey disapproval toward the title character. In fact, the first word with a negative connotation, *impatiently,* does not necessarily indicate that attitude; it is only the follow-up with the word *imperatively* (literally "commanding," but with a connotation of "demanding") here that the reader begins to develop a picture of Editha as someone stubborn and entitled. The narrator's attitude is revealed gradually, as the sentence progresses.

In many cases, the tone and attitude will not be exclusively positive or negative, nor will they remain entirely consistent throughout a passage—more often, it will consist of shifting impressions, and you must be prepared to discuss emotions in a nuanced way. A character may be presented positively in one paragraph and then negatively in the next, or vice versa. The ability to recognize and discuss these complexities is key to earning the "Sophistication" point. **To identify these shifts, focus on transitional words and phrases indicating contrast, e.g., *but*, *yet*, and *however*.**

For example, consider this passage from Nathaniel Hawthorne's novel *The Blithedale Romance,* on which the 2018 Prose Analysis Essay was based.

Shifting: In the gorgeousness with which [Zenobia] had surrounded herself—in the redundance of personal ornament, which the largeness of her physical nature and the rich type of her beauty caused to seem so suitable—I **malevolently beheld the true character of the woman, passionate, luxurious, lacking simplicity, not deeply refined, incapable of pure and perfect taste**.

But, the next instant, she was too powerful for all my opposing struggles. **I saw how fit it was that she should make herself as gorgeous as she pleased, and should do a thousand things that would have been ridiculous in the poor, thin, weakly characters of other.** To this day, **however**, I hardly know whether I then beheld Zenobia in her truest attitude, or whether that were the truer one in which she had presented herself at Blithedale. In both, there was something like the illusion which a great actress flings around her.

Although the narrator spends the entire first paragraph castigating Zenobia for her excessive indulgence, he then pivots and asserts that she should be allowed to do as she wishes ("I saw how fit was that she should make herself as gorgeous as she pleased…"). After that, he shifts direction yet *again*, insisting that he still does not fully understand who Zenobia was. By the end of the second paragraph, his attitude has evolved from bitter denunciation to utter perplexity at his own inability to grasp the situation.

One very common stumbling block for many students involves recognizing humor, irony, and sarcasm. Particularly when passages are written in dense, eighteenth- or nineteenth-century language, this type of non-literal language can be very challenging to identify. Further complicating matters is the fact that the type of humor likely to appear in passages tends to be associated with a negative rather than a positive tone—authors typically employ it to mock or satirize a character's behavior or a situation, not simply to make the reader laugh.

Generally speaking, literary humor revolves around wordplay, the deliberate use of contrast (juxtaposition) between formal and informal, or the gap between what is said and what is actually true.

If you are a strong reader and comfortable with old-fashioned language, you may find it helpful to try to "hear" the text internally as you read, but otherwise you will have to focus on the passage itself. In some cases, authors may go out of their way to provide clues indicating that they are poking fun at someone or something: **quotation marks** (to indicate skepticism, or non-literal usage) and **unusual capitalization** are both common techniques.

For example, consider the following sentence from Edith Wharton's *The Age of Innocence*, which is set among the members of New York's high society in the nineteenth century.

Sarcasm: Few things seemed to Newland Archer more awful than an offence against **"Taste,"** that far-off divinity of whom **"Form"** was the mere visible representative and vicegerent.

In the above sentence, Wharton employs both punctuation techniques, figuratively waving a red flag at the reader to signal that she is mocking the superficial ideals of the upper class.

Let's look at another example from the same novel.

Sarcasm: There was no reason why the young man should not have come [to the opera] earlier, for he had dined at seven, alone with his mother and sister... But, in the first place, New York was a metropolis, and perfectly aware that in metropolises it was **"not the thing"** to arrive early at the opera; **and what was or was not "the thing" played a part as important in Newland Archer's New York as the inscrutable totem terrors that had ruled the destinies of his forefathers thousands of years ago**.

Here again, we have the use of quotation marks, this time around the phrase *(not) the thing* to indicate that Wharton is again poking fun at the seriousness with which certain arbitrary social conventions are treated. In this case, the casual register of the word *thing* also stands in contrast to the rather lofty reference to the opera (symbol of high culture).

Furthermore, the phrase *inscrutable totem terrors that had ruled the destinies of his forefathers thousands of years ago* also serves to make light of the conventions to which Newland is bound—by equating primitive superstitions (low, informal) with the strictures governing Newland's cultured, urbane New York (high, formal), Wharton suggests the absurd amount of weight placed on what are ultimately very low-stakes behaviors. Finally, the over-articulated alliteration in the phrase *totem terrors*, with its emphasis on the "t" sound, invokes a person stuttering in terror—a ridiculous image in this context.

The chart below lists some tone and attitude words that can help you improve the specificity of your analyses.

Positive	Negative		Neutral
Happy Delighted Jovial Sanguine Whimsical **Overjoyed** Ecstatic Effusive Exultant Jubilant **Comical** Amused Irreverent **Modest** Self-deprecating	**Angry** Belligerent Hostile Irate **Arrogant** Condescending Contemptuous Derisive Disdainful Pompous Scornful **Sad** Mournful	**Confused** Ambivalent Bemused Flustered Nonplussed Perplexed **Jealous** Envious Resentful **Nervous** Apprehensive **Sarcastic** Sardonic Facetious	**Objective** Detached Decisive Dispassionate Impartial Reflective **Formal** Stilted **Informal** Casual Conversational

Qualification: Avoiding Extremes

One thing to be aware of is that the language you use to describe the author's tone and the characters' attitudes should be proportionate to the level of extremity in the passage. A common misconception is that a strong analysis is one that includes a lot of dramatic language; however, using dramatic language to describe a passage whose tone is only moderately positive or negative will actually *weaken* your analysis.

When using adjectives to describe tone and attitude, you should therefore use **qualifiers** to indicate the level of intensity. To "qualify" a term means to provide more information about it, usually to soften it or make it less harsh, although sometimes qualification can involve making language more extreme as well.

Mild	Moderate	Extreme
Hardly Marginally Mildly Slightly	Considerably Fairly Moderately More or less Rather Relatively Somewhat	Exceptionally Extraordinarily Extremely Intensely Wildly

Narrative Point of View

There are two main types of narrations that appear on AP Literature passages.

A **first-person narrative** is written from the perspective of the narrator (not to be confused with the author!) and includes the words *I* and *me*.

1st Person: When **I** was a girl **I** went to Bretton about twice a year, and well **I** liked the visit. The house and its inmates specially suited **me**. The large peaceful rooms, the well-arranged furniture, the clear wide windows, the balcony outside, looking down on a fine antique street, where Sundays and holidays seemed always to abide—so quiet was its atmosphere, so clean its pavement—these things pleased **me** well.

Although some older novels may combine a first-person narration with a formal style, on the whole **this type of narrative is more likely to be associated with a less formal, more conversational or confessional tone**.

A **third-person narrative**, on the other hand, is written from an objective perspective (again, not to be confused with the author) and describes other people rather than the narrator him- or herself.

3rd Person: About thirty years ago Miss Maria Ward, of Huntingdon, with only seven thousand pounds, had the good luck to captivate Sir Thomas Bertram, of Mansfield Park, in the county of Northampton, and to be thereby raised to the rank of a baronet's lady, with all the comforts and consequences of an handsome house and large income. All Huntingdon exclaimed on the greatness of the match, and her uncle, the lawyer, himself, allowed her to be at least three thousand pounds short of any equitable claim to it.

Although they may occasionally employ humor or irony, third-person narratives are generally more likely to convey a sense of detachment and formality than are first-person narratives.

Second-person narratives, which address the reader (*you*) directly, do exist, but they are rare, and it is unlikely that you will encounter an AP Literature passage consisting exclusively of this perspective. Sometimes, however, **a first-person or third-person narrator may briefly address the reader directly for dramatic effect**. If you encounter this type of narrative shift, be sure to make a note of it because it will almost certainly occur at a significant point in the passage.

Structuring Your Essay

You have two main options for structuring your essay, and they depend on the organization of the passage itself.

2) By literary device

This is generally the more straightforward option and should be treated as the default.

When you have finished annotating the passage and making note of the various devices it contains, **choose no more than three prominent/significant ones, and devote a paragraph to each**. You should generally limit your discussion to three techniques because anything beyond that will leave you without enough time to develop each point sufficiently.

If there are two prominent techniques that appear throughout the passage, you also can focus on them alone and, if necessary, devote multiple paragraphs to a single one.

Focusing on only one device for the entire essay is risky, however, because you can easily run out of ideas and end up with an essay that is too repetitive. Only go with this choice if you are a strong writer and certain that you have enough material to analyze.

2) Chronologically, in order of the passage

This is an option to consider if the author traces a clear change in a character or relationship over the course of the passage, as opposed to providing a description. Each point (paragraph) can correspond to a key step in the shift—try to choose one place from the beginning, one from the middle, and one from the end.

If you do use this structure, however, you must be careful not to simply narrate the events in the text; each step in your argument must make clear how the passage is moving the characters or action from point A to point B. You should also limit yourself to discussing two, or at most three, of the most important strategies in each section.

The Importance of Making an Outline

It is almost impossible to overstate the importance of spending a few minutes organizing your thoughts on paper before you begin writing, even if you know what your major points are—it is too easy to accidentally veer off course or forget a key point otherwise. Straying from your thesis is a guaranteed way to lose easy points in both the "Commentary and Evidence" and "Sophistication" categories, and having a clear outline will prevent you from falling into that trap.

In addition to your thesis, you should determine your major points/sections, as well as your examples, and have that information present to refer back to as you write. If you make sure in your outline that 1) your thesis clearly responds to the prompt; 2) each point clearly supports your thesis; and 3) each example clearly illustrates the relevant point, your argument will remain focused, and you are more or less guaranteed to score at least 4 out of 6. **Remember: your goal is to be clear and coherent, not brilliant.**

On the next page, we're going to start working with a sample passage.

The following passage is from Edith Wharton's 1905 novel, *The House of Mirth*, which follows the life of a young woman named Lily Bart. In a well-written essay, analyze how the author portrays Selden's attitude toward Lily Bart through the use of literary techniques.

Selden paused in surprise. In the afternoon rush of the Grand Central Station his eyes had been refreshed by the sight of Miss Lily Bart. He was returning to his work from a hurried dip into the country; but what was Miss Bart doing in town? She stood apart from the crowd, letting it drift by her, and wearing an air of irresolution which might, as he surmised, be the mask of a very definite purpose. There was nothing new about Lily Bart, yet **he could never see her without a faint movement of interest: it was characteristic of her that she always roused speculation, that her simplest acts seemed the result of far-reaching intentions.**

An impulse of curiosity made him turn out of his direct line to the door, and stroll past her.

"Mr. Selden—what good luck!"

She came forward smiling, eager almost, in her resolve to intercept him. One or two persons, in brushing past them, lingered to look; for Miss Bart was a figure to arrest even the suburban traveller rushing to his last train.

Selden had never seen her more **radiant**. Her **vivid** head relieved against the **dull** tints of the crowd, made her more conspicuous than in a ball-room, and under her **dark hat and veil** she regained the **girlish smoothness, the purity of tint,** that she was beginning to lose after eleven years of late hours and indefatigable dancing. **Had she indeed reached the nine-and-twentieth birthday with which her rivals credited her?**

"What luck!" she repeated. "How nice of you to come to my rescue!"

He responded joyfully that to do so was his mission in life, and asked what form the rescue was to take.

"Oh, almost any—even to sitting on a bench and talking to me. One sits out a cotillion—why not sit out a train? It isn't a bit hotter here than in Mrs. Van Osburgh's conservatory—and some of the women are not a bit uglier." She broke off, laughing, to explain that she had missed the train to Rhinebeck. "And there isn't another till half-past five." She consulted the little jeweled watch among her laces. "Just two hours to wait. And I don't know what to do with myself. My maid came up this morning, and my aunt's house is closed, and I don't know a soul in town." She glanced plaintively about the station.

"If you can spare the time, do take me somewhere for a breath of air."

He declared himself entirely at her disposal: the adventure struck him as diverting. As a spectator, he had always enjoyed Lily Bart; and his course lay so far out of her orbit that it amused him to be drawn into the sudden intimacy which her proposal implied.

"The resources of New York are rather meagre," he said; "but I'll find a hansom first, and then we'll invent something." He led her through the throng of returning holiday-makers, past sallow-faced girls in preposterous hats, and flat-chested women struggling with paper bundles and palm-leaf fans. **Was it possible that she belonged to the same race?** The **dinginess, the crudity**, of this average section of womanhood made him feel how **highly specialized** she was.

They turned into Madison Avenue and began to stroll northward. As she moved beside him, Selden was conscious of taking a luxurious pleasure in her nearness: in the modelling of her little ear, the crisp upward wave of her hair—**was it ever so slightly brightened by art?**—and the thick planting of her straight black lashes. Everything about her was at once vigorous and exquisite, at once strong and fine. He had a **confused sense** that she must have cost a great deal to make, that a great many dull and ugly people must, in some mysterious way, have been sacrificed to produce her. He was aware that the qualities distinguishing her from the herd of her sex were chiefly external: as though a **fine glaze of beauty and fastidiousness** had been applied to **vulgar clay**. Yet the analogy left him unsatisfied, for a coarse texture will not take a high finish; and **was it not possible that the material was fine, but that circumstance had fashioned it into a futile shape?**

Let's start by just summarizing the passage. Luckily, the action is pretty straightforward: a man named Selden is at the train station when he spots Lily Bart, a woman he knows slightly, and whom he finds intriguing. Lily spots him and tells him that she has missed her train, then asks him to entertain her for a couple of hours while she waits for the next one. He agrees, and they walk together out of the station.

Next, what is the focus of the passage?

Essentially, it's Selden's fascination with the somewhat mysterious Lily. We know that because he indicates his interest both at the end of the first paragraph (*[H]e could never see her without a faint movement of interest: it was characteristic of her that she always roused speculation, that her simplest acts seemed the result of far-reaching intentions.*) and throughout the entire last paragraph. That attitude is also conveyed in a variety of ways throughout the passage.

So that's half the thesis: **the author does x to convey Selden's fascination with Lily.**

Now, we find *x*. In other words, we look at the specific words, punctuation, sentence-structures, etc. that the author uses in order to reveal the narrator's attitude.

If you circled "interesting" punctuation as you read the passage, you might have noticed that there are four question marks, including one in the very last sentence. (You can also just do a quick, purely visual scan of the passage to see whether anything jumps out at you.)

- *Had she indeed reached the nine-and-twentieth birthday with which her rivals credited her?*
- *Was it possible that she belonged to the same race [as the other women Selden sees]?*
- *Selden was conscious of taking a luxurious pleasure in her nearness: in the modelling of her little ear, the crisp upward wave of her hair – was it ever so slightly brightened by art?*
- *[W]as it not possible that the material was fine, but that circumstance had fashioned it into a futile shape?*

The ability to home in on punctuation this way is very important because it offers a straightforward "entry" point into the analysis, one that requires less time and attention to notice than many other devices.

Now, why include all those questions? Well, think about the Selden's attitude toward Lily: he is curious about her – there is something about her he cannot quite pin down. So the questions serve to emphasize that fact.

If we look at the information around the questions, we can actually find a second major technique. Consider, for instance, the paragraph before the first question:

> *Selden had never seen her more* ***radiant****. Her* ***vivid*** *head, relieved against the* ***dull*** *tints of the crowd, made her more conspicuous than in a ball-room, and under her* ***dark hat and veil*** *she regained the* ***girlish smoothness****,* ***the purity of tint****, that she was beginning to lose after eleven years of late hours and indefatigable dancing.*

And the paragraph in which the second question appears:

> *He led her through the throng of returning holiday-makers, past* ***sallow-faced*** *girls in* ***preposterous hats****, and* ***flat-chested women*** *struggling with paper bundles and palm-leaf fans...The* ***dinginess****, the* ***crudity****, of this average section of womanhood made him feel how* ***highly specialized*** *she was.*

Both these sections, as well as the extended description in the final paragraph, make extensive use of **descriptive language** (adjectives) to set up a **contrast** (or **juxtaposition**) between the remarkable Lily Bart and the far more ordinary women that surround her.

This is already lot of material to work with, so we can move to the thesis.

Thesis: Wharton's repeated use of questions as well as a series of highly descriptive contrasts serve to convey Selden's fascination with Lily Bart and depict her as an enigmatic figure.

Note that this is only one possible focus for the essay—there are many other aspects that could be discussed, but given the time constraint, you must decide quickly and stick to your choice!

Having established the thesis, we can now make an outline.

I. Introduction

Present passage - text from HOM, describes encounter betw. Selden + Lily. Selden is intrigued by Lily, wants to know more about her. End w/thesis.

II. Questions

A. Found throughout the passage - convey consistent sense of curiosity

B. Appearance vs. reality: question in 28-30 (is she really 29?)

C. Add'l quotes, reiterate mysterious quality - *was it ever so slightly brightened by art?*

III. Contrast, descriptive language 1

A. Emphasize L.'s extraordinary qualities

B. Lines 22-26 - extremely positive adjectives (radiant, vivid) - Selden is more than a little intrigued.

C. Lines 57-62 - contrast w/other women → more extreme. Very negative.

IV. Contrast, descriptive language 2

A. Final paragraph - Lily is herself a contradiction = mysterious

B. Repetition of *at once,* lines 69-70, emphasizes contradiction

V. Conclusion

Reader absorbs Selden's confusion - no clear idea of who Lily is.

Now let's look at how each part of the essay gets constructed.

Introduction

Because you will have less than 40 minutes to actually write your essay after reading/annotating the passage and (ideally) jotting down a quick outline, you must be able to move through your introduction quickly so that you can focus on the real substance of your analysis in the body paragraphs.

Your primary goal in the introduction is to "set the scene" in order to frame your discussion and orient the reader. It should provide just enough context for your analysis without turning into an extended summary of the passage or a partial analysis. For that reason, you should **try to limit the introduction to around five sentences**.

Note also the use of transitional words and phrases (in bold) to introduce new ideas and keep the reader oriented within the argument.

Step 1: Introduce the situation (1-2 sentences)

In the excerpt from Edith Wharton's novel *The House of Mirth*, a young man named Selden is passing through Grand Central Station when he spots an acquaintance—an intriguing young woman named Lily Bart. The two strike up a conversation, and Lily, who has missed her train, persuades Selden to entertain her for a couple of hours.

Step 2: Transition to your topic (1-2 sentences)

As the passage develops, it becomes clear that Selden views Lily as much more than an ordinary woman. **Indeed**, his words indicate that he finds her utterly exceptional, as well as somewhat mysterious.

Step 3: State your thesis and (optional) introduce examples. (1-2 sentences)

Throughout the text, Wharton uses repeated questions as well as a series of highly descriptive contrasts to convey Selden's fascination with Lily and depict her as an enigmatic figure.

Note that the **narrow scope** of the essay is established right from the beginning—the first couple of sentences indicate that the analysis will focus on the specific events of the passage.

A **less effective** opening, on the other hand, might go something like this:

> Psychology has found that people are often fascinated by individuals that are different from them.

Or:

> Throughout history, some people have always been too mysterious to understand.

Both of these statements are **far too broad**—your essay is not about psychology or mysterious people throughout history, and these statements make your writing seem vague and generic. Remember that you cannot make large generalizations based on characters you are only just encountering for the first time!

Body Paragraphs

At bare minimum, you should **aim for at least five-six sentences** in your body paragraphs, and more if necessary; anything less will not allow for sufficient development, causing you to lose points in the "Evidence and Commentary" category.

As we established in the outline, the first body paragraph will focus on Wharton's use of punctuation, specifically question marks.

Step 1: Transition + topic sentence

From the beginning of the passage, the author takes care to present Lily as a puzzling figure to Selden (we are told in line 12 that she "always roused speculation"), and one of the most striking ways in which she emphasizes this quality is through the use of questions.

Step 2: Introduce quotation(s)

For example, in lines 28-29 Selden wonders whether Lily "had indeed reached the nine-and-twentieth birthday with which her rivals credited her."

Step 3: Analyze examples and explain their significance

It is significant that the narrator does not state Lily's age outright **but instead** presents it more ambiguously. Like Selden, we do not know for certain that she is nearly 30 (an old maid by 1905 standards!). **Rather**, this aspect of her identity is merely hinted at. <u>By introducing us to Lily in this manner, Wharton establishes the character herself as a sort of question mark, someone who perhaps is not entirely what she appears to be.</u>

Do not forget the second step, underlined above—quotations do not explain themselves! You must **explicitly** state the implications of your evidence; do not assume that the reader can put the pieces together.

Step 4: If necessary, repeat steps 2 and 3

This impression is affirmed as Selden observes Lily while they are walking out of the station: observing the "upward wave of her hair," he asks himself, "was it ever so slightly brightened by art?" (lines 67-68). With these words, the narrator again subtly suggests that Lily's youthful appearance is something of a mirage. <u>**Interestingly**, this ambiguity makes her no less alluring to Selden; **in fact**, he finds her all the more entrancing for it, taking "luxurious pleasure in her nearness."</u>

Again, notice how the quotation is not simply left hanging. Both the second and third sentences comment on it, not by merely restating what it says in descriptive language (a very common trap) but rather by using it to push the analysis forward.

Now let's look at the rest of the sample essay in regular form. Notice how **quotations are never just dropped in without a discussion afterward**. Rather, specific aspects of them are discussed and used to advance the analysis. Notice also the **consistent use of transitions** to orient the reader within the argument.

Rest of the essay:

Throughout the passage, the narrator's consistent use of contrast when describing Lily Bart is striking **as well. If** the repeated questions emphasize her elusive quality, **then** the opposing pairs of adjectives serve to both reinforce this idea and emphasize her contradictory nature—**as well as** the extraordinary impression she makes in comparison to other, more ordinary individuals. **For example**, in lines 22-26, in which Selden observes Lily up close for the first time, the narrator describes her as "radiant" and "vivid," adjectives that contrast sharply with the "dull tints of the crowd." **Here**, Lily is established as a sort of beacon, shining above the faceless masses—in Selden's perception, at least.

As the paragraph progresses, however, the contradiction shifts onto Lily herself: her "dark hat and veil" (obvious symbols of ageing) are juxtaposed with her "girlish smoothness, [her] purity of tint." **Like** the question that follows, this image serves to suggest the distance between appearance and reality, and to imply that the face Lily presents to the world is perhaps no longer representative of who she truly is. That idea is presented only fleetingly here, **however**, and is not returned to until the end of the passage—almost as if the narrator were teasing the reader with it. **In the meantime**, the narrator takes care to underline the gap between Lily and the women who surround her, most notably in lines 56-59. **As the narrator describes**, Selden "led [Lily] through the throng of returning holiday-makers, past sallow-faced girls in preposterous hats, and flat-chested women struggling with paper bundles and palm-leaf fans." By presenting the other women in the station as exaggeratedly unattractive ("sallow-faced"), asexual ("flat-chested"), quasi-ridiculous figures (their hats are "preposterous"), presumably as Selden sees them, the narrator implies the extent to which he idealizes (and idolizes) Lily.

It is in the final paragraph of the passage that Selden's attitude becomes less straightforwardly worshipful and more ambiguous—and ambivalent. **In particular**, the repetition of "at once" and the use of antithesis ("vigorous" vs. "exquisite"; "strong" vs. "fine") in lines 69-70, as well as the opposition between "fine glaze of beauty and fastidiousness" and "vulgar clay" in lines 76-77, create the impression of a woman composed of a mass of contradictions. **Indeed**, the narrator's reference to Selden's "confused sense" further emphasizes her destabilizing effect on him. **As the paragraph moves on**, Selden's thoughts begin to reflect this confusion: in the last few lines, he is unable to even form a clear analogy to explain to himself the qualities that distinguish Lily from "the herd of her sex." The narrator's use of the word "herd" is particularly crude, suggesting that Selden is becoming increasingly carried away. Clearly, this is no simple infatuation.

Conclusion

Your conclusion does not need to be particularly long, and in fact, if your final body paragraph ends on a sufficiently strong note, you may not need a separate conclusion at all.

That said, if you do want to include one, you can aim for about three or four sentences—just enough to finish things off without seeming overly abrupt.

Step 1: Transition from the previous paragraph

It is unsurprising, then, that the passage should end with an uneasy question about which aspects of Lily are superficial and which are genuine. Is she merely a beautiful façade hiding something far less attractive, or does the exterior reflect the interior?

Step 2: Tie it back to the thesis.

Through this final gesture, the author conveys the extent of Lily's sheer magnetism and enchanting quality, as well as her elusive and contradictory nature.

Step 3: Finish it off.

Like Selden himself, the reader is left with a question: who, truly, is Lily Bart?

The Elements of Style

Now, having considered the big picture, we're going to look at some general stylistic issues. While you will not lose points for minor spelling or grammatical errors, repeated and flagrant mistakes will give your readers an impression of sloppiness and make it difficult for them to follow your argument.

Tense Consistency

As a general rule, **use the literary present when discussing works of literature**.

Incorrect: In Cormac McCarthy's The Road, the protagonists' commitment to each other **was** tested in dangerous and life-threatening situations, but they **found** a way to stick together. They **overlooked** each other's mistakes and **were** able to move forward because they **knew** that holding a grudge or going separate ways would lead to their demise.

Correct: In Cormac McCarthy's The Road, the protagonists' commitment to each other **is** tested in dangerous and life-threatening situations, but they **find** a way to stick together. They **overlook** each other's mistakes and **are** able to move forward because they **know** that holding a grudge or going separate ways will lead to their demise.

Only use the past tense to discuss events that clearly occurred prior to the action of the story.

Correct: McCarthy creates a world barren of life, except for the few who **managed** to survive the catastrophe that has left the earth devoid of natural resources.

Note that the past perfect (*had + verb*) indicates a finished action in the past that came **before** a second finished action. As a result, this tense should not generally be used.

Passive Voice

In an **active** construction, the subject of a sentence typically comes before the object. The emphasis is on the person or thing performing the action.

William Shakespeare	wrote	*Hamlet*.
subject	**verb**	**object**

In a **passive** construction, however, the subject and the object are flipped. The passive voice also includes a form of the verb *to be + past participle* and the preposition *by*. As a result, *x did y* becomes *y was done by x*. The emphasis is on the object as the receiver of the action.

Hamlet	was written	by	William Shakespeare.
subject	**verb**	**preposition**	**object**

Although the passive voice is commonly treated as something of a grammatical punching bag, there are times when it is perfectly appropriate for a given situation, e.g., to indicate that something is being done *to* a character.

Acceptable: In Kate Chopin's "The Story of an Hour," the protagonist **is confined** to the traditional role of wife and mother **by** both her husband and nineteenth-century American society as a whole.

In this case, the use of the passive voice makes sense because it serves to emphasize that the protagonist is on the receiving end of the action.

On the other hand, the repeated and indiscriminate use of the passive can create constructions that are unnecessarily wordy and awkward.

Awkward: In "The Story of an Hour," the emotions of a woman who is married and uncomfortably confined to her role of wife and mother **are described by Kate Chopin**. The customs of American society in the nineteenth century **are depicted by the author**, and a story that accurately reflects the experiences of many women of that time **is created by her**.

In the above example, the repeated use of the passive bogs the prose down. In contrast, the active verbs in the version below make the prose cleaner and easier to absorb.

Clear: In "The Story of an Hour," **Kate Chopin describes** the emotions of a woman who is married and uncomfortably confined to her role of wife and mother. **The author depicts** the customs of American society in the nineteenth century and **creates** a story that accurately reflects the experiences of many women of that time.

Use Verbs and Nouns, Not -ING Words (Gerunds)

Another way to strengthen your writing is to avoid the unnecessary use of -ING words (gerunds). Like the passive, this construction can easily become awkward and weigh down your writing.

Awkward: **Because of the narrator's <u>believing</u>** that no one could possibly thwart his attempt to find literary gold, he exhibits an excessive amount of confidence.

Clear: **Because the narrator <u>believes</u>** that no one could possibly thwart his attempt to find literary gold, he exhibits an excessive amount of confidence.

Clear: **Because of the narrator's <u>belief</u>** that no one could possibly thwart his attempt to find literary gold, he exhibits an excessive amount of confidence.

"Vague" Pronouns

Another common trap involves pronouns like *this*, *that*, and *what*.

Although it is fine to use these words without a noun or phrase afterward, you should be very careful to limit your reliance on this construction because it can easily make your writing seem vague and overly casual.

Vague: Conflict and human experience are necessary ingredients in a great novel. The passage from A Farewell to Arms contains both of **these**. **This** causes the reader to become intrigued about **what will happen**.

Specific: Conflict and human experience are necessary ingredients in a great novel. The passage from A Farewell to Arms contains both of **these elements, causing the reader to become intrigued about how the plot will develop**.

To reiterate, statements beginning with *what* are particularly ambiguous.

Vague: In the novel Middlemarch, Dorothea Brooke becomes unhappy because of **what she does**.

Instead of just referring to "what she does," you need to **explicitly state** what she did—do not force your reader to guess.

Specific: In the novel Middlemarch, Dorothea Brooke becomes unhappy because of **her decision to marry the dull and scholarly Mr. Casaubon.**

Using Transitions Effectively

Transitional words and phrases indicate whether you are presenting evidence, moving to a new example, or drawing a conclusion. They serve as "signposts" that help readers orient themselves in your argument, and their effective use is crucial to achieving a high score.

Example 1: Initially, Selden's attitude toward Lily is primarily one of curiosity, but as the passage progresses, he becomes increasingly entranced by her charms.

Example 2: Throughout the passage, the repetition of the word "forever" conveys the depth of the narrator's longing. **Moreover,** it creates a timeless quality, as if the action were occurring outside the constraints of the everyday world.

Example 3: The House of Mirth depicts the intricate art of keeping up appearances and maintaining one's status within the leisure class. **At the same time**, it subtly critiques this social order.

One simple way to make your writing sound more sophisticated is to place an occasional transition in the middle of a sentence rather than at the beginning.

Beginning: Throughout the passage, Melville includes images related to sailors and the sea; **however,** he also employs a variety of other techniques, including repetition and alliteration.

Middle: Throughout the passage, Melville includes images related to sailors and the sea. He also**, however,** employs a variety of other techniques, including repetition and alliteration.

In both sentences, the transition serves exactly the same purpose: to connect the second statement to the first. Version 2 simply moves the transition to a less-expected location, making the sentence more interesting stylistically.

Continuers		Contradictors
Support, Illustrate, Bolster, Provide Evidence Also And As well as Furthermore For example For instance In addition Moreover One reason/another reason **Indicate Sequence of Events** Previously First/In the first place Initially Presently In short order Next Then Soon Subsequently Eventually In the end Finally Ultimately	**Explain, Clarify, Define** Effectively Essentially In other words Properly speaking That is **Cause and Effect** Accordingly As a result As such Because Consequently For Hence So Therefore Thus Thereby To these ends **Compare** Likewise (Just) as Much as/like More/Less...than Similarly	**Refute, Criticize, Challenge, Dispute, Contrast** (Al)though/Even though Alternately/Alternatively But Conversely Despite However In contrast In spite of Instead Nevertheless On the contrary On one hand On the other hand Otherwise Still Regardless Rather than Whereas While Yet

Vary Your Sentence-Structure

Varying the structure of your sentences makes your writing seem livelier and more interesting.

Boring: There are several themes present in the excerpt from Fielding's Tom Jones. One important theme involves the conflict between parental authority and individual choice in matters of love and marriage. In the passage, characters often express ideas about love to other characters. When they do this, they also raise questions about autonomy and self-determination.

The above paragraph is acceptable, but on a stylistic level, it's fairly dull. Compare it to this version, which flows much more effectively.

Interesting: Among the themes present in the excerpt from Fielding's Tom Jones, one of the most important ones involves the conflict between parental authority and individual choice in matters of love and marriage. When characters express their ideas about love—as occurs frequently in the passage—they also raise questions about autonomy and self-determination.

Avoid Repetition

One common pitfall to avoid involves latching onto a particular word and using it repeatedly. In addition to making your writing seem simplistic stylistically, excessive repetition can also prevent you from developing your analysis and obtaining the "Sophistication" point.

Repetitive: In "Editha," William Dean Howells tells the story of an **idealistic** young girl who manipulates her fiancé, George, into going off to war. Throughout Editha's interactions with George, Howells demonstrates how **idealism** can lead a person to develop unethical **ideals**. Editha's **idealistic** view of war leads her to underestimate its dangers, and readers are taught the importance of loving someone for who they are.

There's nothing wrong with the word "idealistic," but using a version of it four times in three sentences is excessive. Compare it to this version, which uses four separate terms.

Varied: In "Editha," William Dean Howells tells the story of an **idealistic** young girl who manipulates her fiancé, George, into going off to war. Throughout Editha's interactions with George, Howells demonstrates how **excessive romanticism** can lead a person to develop unethical **principles**. Editha's **naive** view of war leads her to underestimate its dangers, and readers are taught the importance of loving someone for who they are.

Now the paragraph contains a mix of sentence types and punctuation. What was originally four sentences is now two, one of which is broken up by a dash ("interesting" punctuation). Compared to the previous version, this reads much more smoothly and is more engaging.

One area in which it is particularly easy to become repetitive involves introducing quotations.

The verbs *say* and *states* are typically the default options for introducing direct citations from the text, but you should attempt to find more colorful, precise alternatives whenever possible.

Boring: In lines 31-32, Lily **says**, "How nice of you to come to my rescue!"

Interesting: In lines 31-32, Lily **exclaims**, "How nice of you to come to my rescue!"

The list below provides a range of options.

• asserts	• implies
• calls attention to	• indicates
• claims	• insinuates
• confirms	• insists
• contends	• points out
• describes	• reiterates
• emphasizes	• reveals
• exclaims	• suggests
• explains	• underlines
• illustrates	• underscores

It is important to avoid repetition at the paragraph level as well.

Once you have introduced a point, move on to another part of your argument (citing from the text, tying it back to your thesis, etc.)—while you may want to reiterate the point once, and ideally from a slightly different angle, after you have finished your analysis, **repeating your point throughout a paragraph is not a substitute for analyzing the text**.

Repetitive: Kate Chopin was a writer who **wrote to depict obstacles** and instances occurring **within her time period**. **Writing about personal obstacles**, as well as issues occurring **in the time period she lived**, Chopin proved to be an **ambitious individual**. Kate Chopin was a determined author, with **true ambition** and ability to produce writings that placed a higher value on women's experiences and **the obstacles they overcame**.

Notice that the argument here never progresses—the writer simply repeats the same point over and over. Compare it to the version below.

Stronger: Kate Chopin was a writer who wrote to depict obstacles and instances occurring within her time period. **As a woman in the nineteenth century, she was preoccupied with the restrictions imposed on her gender and ambitiously sought to depict the reality of women's lives.**

Register and Conventions

Register refers to how **formal** or **informal** a writer's language is. The Prose Analysis Essay must be written in the same **moderately formal style** as any paper you would write for English class and observe the same conventions of standard written English.

Avoid casual language.

Casual: Edna Pontellier, the novel's heroine, is a wife and mother of two **little kids**.

Correct: Edna Pontellier, the novel's heroine, is a wife and mother of two **young children**.

All words should be written out (with the exception of titles that are normally abbreviated, e.g., Dr. and Mr.). Do not use ampersands (& signs) or other abbreviations.

Incorrect: In Kate Chopin's novel The Awakening, Edna Pontellier demonstrates her newfound **passion & independence** through painting.

Correct: In Kate Chopin's novel The Awakening, Edna Pontellier demonstrates her newfound **passion and independence** through painting.

Write out numbers smaller than 10.

Incorrect: At the beginning of The Awakening, Edna Pontellier is a happy woman with a husband and **2 children**, vacationing at Grand Isle.

Correct: At the beginning of The Awakening, Edna Pontellier is a happy woman with a husband and **two children**, vacationing at Grand Isle.

Refer to authors by their last names.

Incorrect: In The Awakening, **Kate** depicts the liberation and subsequent downfall of Edna Pontellier, a wife and a mother who rebels against her socially prescribed role.

Correct: In The Awakening, **Chopin** depicts the liberation and subsequent downfall of Edna Pontellier, a wife and a mother who rebels against her socially prescribed role.

Titles of literary works should be capitalized.

Incorrect: In Kate Chopin's novel **the awakening**, Edna Pontellier, a wife and a mother, rebels against her socially prescribed role, with tragic results.

Correct: In Kate Chopin's novel **The Awakening**, Edna Pontellier, a wife and a mother, rebels against her socially prescribed role, with tragic results.

Diction

In addition to being able to analyze this aspect of the text effectively, you must also maintain control over your own vocabulary in order to convey your ideas clearly. In particular, make sure to know the differences between these commonly confused pairs of words.

Imply vs. Infer

Imply - suggest. The writer implies something *to* the reader.

Infer - draw a conclusion based on unstated information. The reader infers the meaning *from* what the author has (not) written.

Incorrect: In his short story "Editha," Howells **infers** that an excessively idealistic mindset can lead people to adopt unethical principles.

Correct: In his short story "Editha," Howells **implies** that an excessively idealistic mindset can lead people to adopt unethical principles.

Denote vs. Connote

Denotation - literal definition of a word.

Connotation - (non-literal) implication of a word or image.

Incorrect: Throughout the passage, the image of smoke **denotes** confusion and uncertainty.

Correct: Throughout the passage, the image of smoke **connotes** confusion and uncertainty.

Beyond correct use of these pairs, one of the key differences between lower- and higher-scoring essays is the level of vocabulary they employ. Although it is unnecessary to flood your writing with "ten-dollar" words, a handful of moderately sophisticated terms will make your work seem more polished. In particular, the use of strong and specific verbs will make your analyses clearer and more precise.

Weaker: The novel Silas Marner, written by George Eliot, contains two characters who **cross paths with one another**. Silas Marner, a **poor** old man, is framed for a crime **that wasn't his fault**. With no evidence **to back him up**, Silas **gets kicked out** of his hometown, forcing him to stay in Raveloe. However, his luck **gets better** when he adopts a young girl, Eppie, who helps him **learn to believe in others again**.

Like some of the other "adequate" versions we've seen, this paragraph is fine—it's just not stellar. While it gets its point across, it does not include a particularly challenging vocabulary.

Now, compare the previous version to the version below, which organically weaves in a handful of more sophisticated terms without going overboard.

Stronger: The novel Silas Marner, written by George Eliot, contains two characters whose paths **become intertwined**. Silas Marner, a **destitute** old man, is framed for a crime **he did not commit**. With no evidence to **exonerate** him, Silas **is exiled from** his hometown, forcing him to stay in Raveloe. However, his luck **improves** when he adopts a young girl, Eppie, who helps him **regain his faith in others**.

At the same time, you should not get carried away. Although it might impress your English teacher, excessively flowery or verbose writing should be avoided because it detracts from the reader's ability to follow your argument. You are commenting on a piece of literature, not *writing* a piece of literature.

The second example below, for instance, combines sophisticated yet precise vocabulary with an effective use of transitions to keep the reader oriented and move them logically from point to point within the argument.

Excessive: In The Mayor of Casterbridge, the characters' duplicity, though well-intentioned, forms a tent-flap of emotional insurance around their lives, a flimsy fabric of fleeting tranquility threatening to cave in at the slightest whim of a rumorous wind.

Clear: In The Mayor of Casterbridge, the characters' duplicity, though well-intentioned, serves only to insulate them emotionally. **Ultimately, however**, that mask is flimsy and does nothing to protect them. **Indeed**, it reveals their fragility, **for*** they become psychologically destabilized at the slightest hint of trouble.

A related issue involves the misconception that an easy way to score points is to offer effusive praise for the author. While the writer of the passage may very well have been renowned, brilliant, etc., pointing out this information in overblown language will weaken your essay.

Avoid: Kate Chopin was a **determined and brilliant writer, with exceptional ambition and an extraordinary ability** to produce novels that rescued women from the debased state into which nineteenth-century society placed them.

**For* is used to mean "because" here.

Working with Quotations

One of the factors taken into account for both your "Commentary and Evidence" and "Sophistication" scores is your ability to cite the passage effectively. Because the Prose Analysis Essay requires you to cite extensively, you should be comfortable punctuating both direct and indirect quotations, and integrating them naturally into your analysis.

- In **direct speech**, a person's words are presented directly. Quotation marks are used.
- In **indirect speech**, the writer restates a person's words. No quotation marks are used.

Direct: For example, Robert Cohn asks Jake, **"Don't you ever get the feeling that all your life is going by and you're not taking advantage of it?"**

Indirect: For example, Robert Cohn asks Jake **whether he ever gets the feeling that all his life is going by without him taking advantage of it.**

Notice that in the "indirect" version, no quotation marks are used because Robert Cohn's words have been **rephrased** by the writer.

When the word *that* is used to set off an indirect quotation, no comma is placed after it.

Incorrect: When Lana Lee is initially unable to persuade Jones to take his glasses off, she repeats **that, she** told him to remove his glasses.

Correct: When Lana Lee is initially unable to persuade Jones to take his glasses off, she repeats **that she** told him to remove his glasses.

Likewise, when a direct quotation is integrated directly into a sentence, no comma is used.

Incorrect: Physically hidden behind his glasses and metaphorically hidden behind his stereotype, Jones skillfully escapes any interpretation by Lana Lee, who sees him only **as, "the** cloud of smoke and the broom."

Correct: Physically hidden behind his glasses and metaphorically hidden behind his stereotype, Jones skillfully escapes any interpretation by Lana Lee, who sees him only **as "the** cloud of smoke and the broom."

To condense a quotation, use **ellipses** (three dots) to show that material has been left out.

Correct: The blinds of the King's Arms hotel are deliberately left open so that outsiders and passersby can view the "babble of voices **and...the** drawing of corks."

If you change a word or phrase in order to integrate a quotation into a sentence, the altered information should be placed in **brackets**.

Correct: Henry's devotion to Catherine is evident when he repeatedly says that "if **[she isn't] with [him], [he]** hasn't a thing in the world."

Make sure to introduce your quotations—do not simply drop them into the text without warning!

No intro: Editha's fiancé, George, is a committed pacifist as a result of his upbringing. However, Editha believes that war is glorious and that George enlisting would be a symbol of his love to her. **"[I]f he could do something worthy to have won her—be a hero, her hero..."**

The point of the quote is clear enough, but the writer does nothing to let the reader know it's coming. Compare it to this version, which integrates the quotation smoothly into the analysis.

Intro: Editha's fiancé, George, is a committed pacifist as a result of his upbringing. However, Editha believes that war is glorious and that George's enlisting in the army would be a symbol of his love to her. **Caught in her own fantasy, she muses, "if he could do something worthy to have won her—be a hero, her hero..."**

Here, the quote is integrated much more naturally into the surrounding text. It is no longer necessary for the reader to stop and reorient themselves within the argument.

Now let's look at what happens after the quotation.

Weaker: However, Editha believes that war is glorious and that George's enlisting in the army would be a symbol of his love to her. Caught in her own fantasy, she muses, "if he could do something worthy to have won her—be a hero, her hero..." **As the reader discovers, however, George is willing to do whatever it takes to please Editha, and she knows this too.**

The main thing to notice here is that once the quotation is finished, the writer does not engage with it further but rather moves on to the next idea—namely, that George compromises his ideals to please Editha. The essay does not suffer inordinately; however, the writer misses an excellent opportunity to explore some subtleties of the text.

To reiterate: no matter how obvious their significance may seem to you, quotations do not explain themselves—and to earn a high score in "Evidence and Commentary," you must make the relationship between your examples and your argument clear. Even if your evidence is very strong and your analysis is otherwise on target, failure to comment on quotations will knock your score in this category from a 4 to a 3.

To move your argument to a more sophisticated level, you can use a quote as a sort of "springboard" that allows you to add more depth to your analysis. **Note that this does not mean *rephrasing* the quotation in fancier language. Rather, it involves considering its language, punctuation, etc., and using those specific features to support a larger point.**

For example, consider the repetition of the word *hero* as well as the use of ellipses afterward. An analysis that focused on these features might look like the following example.

Stronger: ...However, Editha believes that war is glorious and that George's enlisting in the army would be a symbol of his love to her. Caught in her own fantasy, she muses, "if he could do something worthy to have won her—be a hero, her hero..." **Here, the repetition of the word "hero" serves to underscore Editha's naively romantic tendencies; moreover, the use of ellipses imply a sort of drifting off, emphasizing the daydreamy, almost cartoonish quality of her thoughts. The reader can very nearly imagine a thought-bubble appearing over Editha's head, filled with technicolor images of George returning triumphantly from the war to sweep her off her feet. But ridiculous as this image may be, its ultimate effect is to convey the tragic extent of Editha's self-involvement: she is willing to allow a man who genuinely loves her to sacrifice himself for her fantasy.**

The Text Must Directly Support Your Analysis

Although this is not technically a stylistic consideration, it bears reiterating here: One of the most common traps students fall into in their analyses involves extrapolating far beyond what the passage directly implies. Let's return to the *House of Mirth* passage. A typical example would go something like the excerpt below.

Too far: ...The narrator states that Lily "consulted the little jeweled watch among her laces" and that her "maid came up this morning." **This shows that Lily comes from a very wealthy background and has an haughty and condescending manner. Clearly, she looks down on Selden and perceives him as her social inferior.**

While these details certainly paint Lily as privileged—and the passage implies elsewhere that she is something of a party girl—the information cited simply does not support this interpretation, and you cannot project your own assumptions onto the text.

Now consider this version.

Stronger: ...The narrator states that Lily "consulted the little jeweled watch among her laces" and that her "maid came up this morning." **With this description, Wharton alludes to Lily's elevated social status without mentioning it directly, subtly explaining why Lily has managed to maintain such a frivolous lifestyle despite being at the limits of marriageable age. It also calls attention to the difference in class between Lily and Selden.**

In contrast to the previous example, the above paragraph keeps the analysis squarely within the bounds of the text.

In the next section, we're going to look at three original, full-length sample essays, accompanied by detailed scoring analyses. The first two essays are based on the passage from the 2018 exam, and the third is based on the passage from the 2019 exam.

Although I am including the passages, I suggest that you try reading the essays on their own first. The mark of a successful essay is that it can stand on its own—that is, a reader can easily follow the argument even if they are unfamiliar with the passage. See whether you can do that as you read.

Please note that essays are reprinted with original errors.

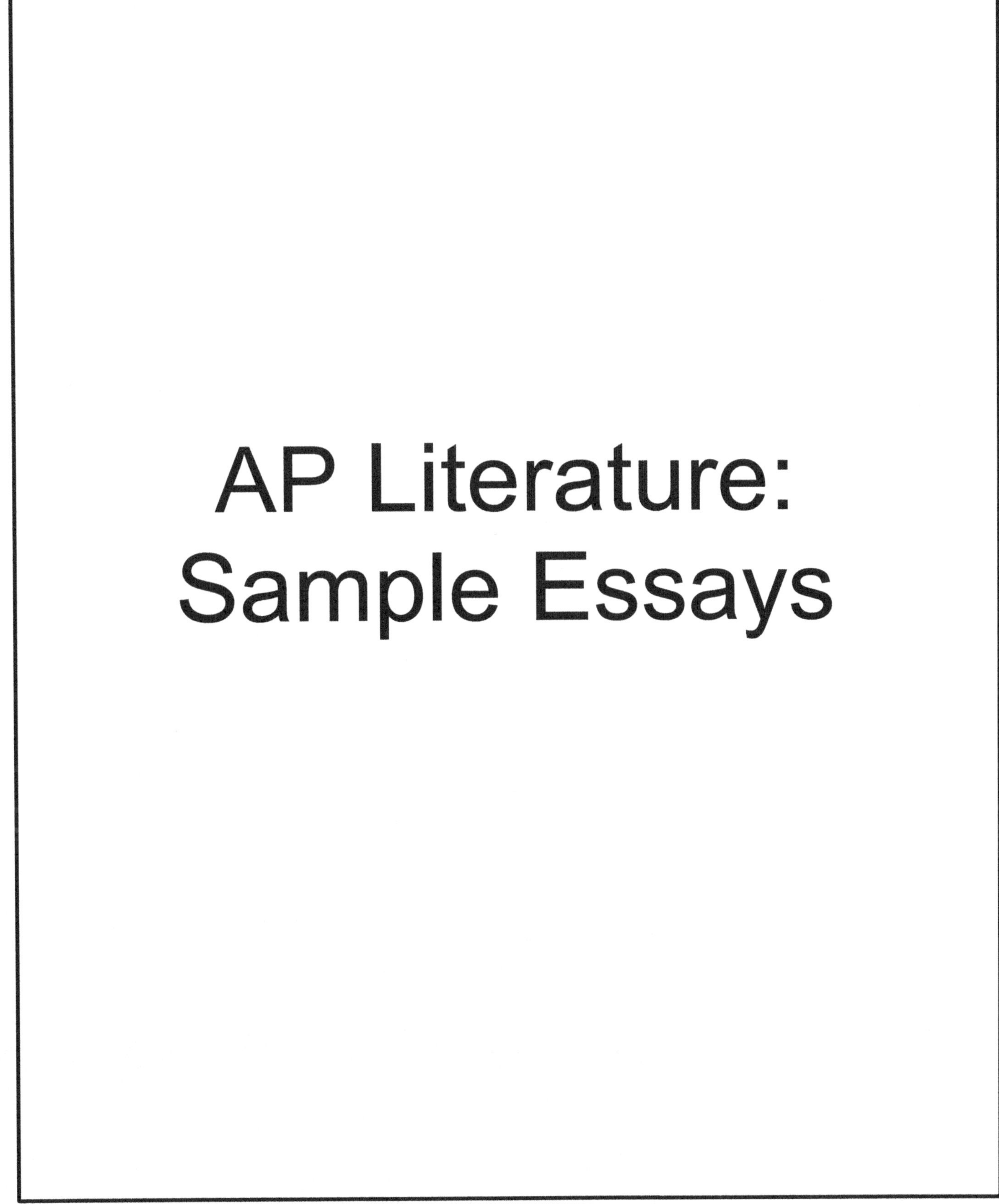

AP Literature: Sample Essays

Passage 1 (from *The Blithedale Romance* by Nathaniel Hawthorne; 2019 Exam)

Her manner bewildered me. Literally, moreover, I was dazzled by the brilliancy of the room. A chandelier hung down in the centre, glowing with I know not how many lights; there were separate lamps, also, on two or three tables, and on marble brackets, adding their white radiance to that of the chandelier. The furniture was exceedingly rich. Fresh from our old farm-house, with its homely board and benches in the dining-room, and a few wicker chairs in the best parlor, it struck me that here was the fulfillment of every fantasy of an imagination, revelling in various methods of costly self-indulgence and splendid ease. Pictures, marbles, vases; in brief, more shapes of luxury than there could be any object in enumerating, except for an auctioneer's advertisement—and the whole repeated and doubled by the reflection of a great mirror, which showed me Zenobia's proud figure, likewise, and my own. It cost me, I acknowledge, a bitter sense of shame, to perceive in myself a positive effort to bear up against the effect which Zenobia sought to impose on me. I reasoned against her, in my secret mind, and strove so to keep my footing. In the gorgeousness with which she had surrounded herself — in the redundance of personal ornament, which the largeness of her physical nature and the rich type of her beauty caused to seem so suitable I malevolently beheld the true character of the woman, passionate, luxurious, lacking simplicity, not deeply refined, incapable of pure and perfect taste.

But, the next instant, she was too powerful for all my opposing struggles. I saw how fit it was that she should make herself as gorgeous as she pleased, and should do a thousand things that would have been ridiculous in the poor, thin, weakly characters of other women. To this day, however, I hardly know whether I then beheld Zenobia in her truest attitude, or whether that were the truer one in which she had presented herself at Blithedale. In both, there was something like the illusion which a great actress flings around her.

"Have you given up Blithedale forever?" I inquired.

"Why should you think so?" asked she.

"I cannot tell," answered I; "except that it appears all like a dream that we were ever there together."

"It is not so to me," said Zenobia. "I should think it a poor and meagre nature, that is capable of but one set of forms, and must convert all the past into a dream, merely because the present happens to be unlike it. Why should we be content with our homely life of a few months past, to the exclusion of all other modes? It was good; but there are other lives as good or better. Not, you will understand, that I condemn those who give themselves up to it more entirely than I, for myself, should deem it wise to do."

It irritated me, this self-complacent, condescending, qualified approval and criticism of a system to which many individuals — perhaps as highly endowed as our gorgeous Zenobia — had contributed their all of earthly endeavor, and their loftiest aspirations. I determined to make proof if there were any spell that would exorcise her out of the part which she seemed to be acting. She should be compelled to give me a glimpse of something true; some nature, some passion, no matter whether right or wrong, provided it were real.

"Your allusion to that class of circumscribed characters, who can live in only one mode of life," remarked I, coolly, "reminds me of our poor friend Hollingsworth. Possibly, he was in your thoughts, when you spoke thus. Poor fellow! It is a pity that, by the fault of a narrow education, he should have so completely immolated himself to that one idea of his; especially as the slightest modicum of common-sense would teach him its utter impracticability. Now that I have returned into the world, and can look at his project from a distance, it requires quite all my real regard for this respectable and well-intentioned man to prevent me laughing at him — as, I find, society at large does!"

Zenobia's eyes darted lightning; her cheeks flushed; the vividness of her expression was like the effect of a powerful light, flaming up suddenly within her. My experiment had fully succeeded. She had shown me the true flesh and blood of her heart, by thus involuntarily resenting my slight, pitying, half- kind, half-scornful mention of the man who was all in all with her. She herself, probably, felt this; for it was hardly a moment before she tranquillized her uneven breath, and seemed as proud and self-possessed as ever.

Sample Essay #1

In the "Blithedale" passage by Nathanial Hawthorne writes about the narrator's attitude towards Zenobia. **The passage is written from the first-person perspective, using imagery of opulence and analytical dialogue that indicates the narrator's first feeling of bewilderment which develops into contempt towards Zenobia.**

The first person perspective gives insight into the current events of the passage, the character awestruck by the abundance of wealth in the room, which is in contrast with the "farm-house, with its homely board and benches", that the narrator and Zenobia are coming from before. The imagery of the grand mirror, repeating and doubling this opulence shows Zenobia's figure that is basking in the wealth. The narrator observes how he is shameful of this wealth while Zenobia is prideful in her surroundings, describing to himself her switch of behavior. "I malevolently beheld the true character of the woman, passionate, luxurious, lacking simplicity, not deeply refined, incapable of pure and perfect taste". The narrator continues by describing Zenobia's prideful behavior "self-complacent, condescending, qualified approval and criticism" towards him, though they have both lived together in a rural commune. The internal thoughts and responses the narrator has towards Zenobia shift throughout the passage which the audience can understand where the feelings of disdain arise from. The first-person narration gives the central insight of the narrator's mind which exhibits the shift of attitude towards Zenobia.

Additionally, the visual of opulence is described throughout the passage strings along with the feelings of bewilderment to contempt. In the passage, Zenobia and the narrator come from the same humble living arrangements—a commune. This was a place that prompted the ideology of communalism, simple living, and sharing what little the community had. The room is the exact opposite of this, with "exceedingly rich furniture", "many lights", "three separate tables on marble brackets", "chandelier hanging down the center", and a glittering mirror. All these indicate the conflicting morals the narrator holds towards simple living, while Zenobia is absorbed into the room's gilded appearance. The narrator is taken aback by this apparent wealthy lifestyle Zenobia now lives, shifting his perspective on the women he used to know from the commune. This juxtaposes the life before to the life after the commune, showing the narrator he does not truly know Zenobia as he once did before.

Finally, the analytical dialogue that takes place between Zenobia and the narrator solidifies the narrator's feelings. The start of the passage explores the narrator's bewilderment of Zenobia's mannerism which then advances into his component for her pridefulness and vanity. The exchange between the characters displays their differences as the narrator rebuttals at Zenobia's comment about "commending those who give themselves up" to a more humble lifestyle. The narrator mentions their mutual friend, Hollingsworth, and how Zenobia must have been referencing him and others like him living in Blithedale. How they are laughed at by society at large, which would include Zenobia and her current position in society. Zenobia's physical reaction "eyes darted", "cheeks flushed", "flaming up", shows her true personality. The narrator is now solidified in Zenobia's prideful personality, her back turned on the people of her past community, and her superficial character. His attitude towards her is forever changed and he has lost all respect for her. The usage of first-person narration, imagery, and analytical dialogue, Hawthrone depicts the narrator's initial bewilderment and eventual contempt regarding Zenobia.

Score: 5/6

Thesis: 1/1

The essay earns a point in this category because it makes a defensible claim: *The passage is written from the first-person perspective, using imagery of opulence and analytical dialogue that indicates the narrator's first feeling of bewilderment which develops into contempt towards Zenobia.*

Evidence and Commentary: 3/4

On the whole, the writer effectively supports the argument with clear evidence from the passage. The body paragraphs are logically arranged in two parts, with the first part (paragraphs 2 and 3) corresponding to imagery of opulence and the second part (paragraph 4) corresponding to analytical dialogue. Within the body paragraphs, the writer offers extended commentary on the quotations, e.g., *The imagery of the grand mirror, repeating and doubling this opulence shows Zenobia's figure that is basking in the wealth. The narrator observes how he is shameful of this wealth while Zenobia is prideful in her surroundings, describing to himself her switch of behavior,* and *All these indicate the conflicting morals the narrator holds towards simple living, while Zenobia is absorbed into the room's gilded appearance.*

Despite the generally strong analysis, the third paragraph loses focus somewhat. Although it begins strongly, by reiterating the thesis (*Additionally, the visual of opulence is described throughout the passage strings along with the feelings of bewilderment to contempt*), the relationship between the discussion of communalism and "bewilderment" is not fully explained, nor is it reflected in the choice of quotations. In addition, the final paragraph is somewhat short on direct quotations: the writer alludes to the narrator's dialogue with Zenobia but does not cite from it directly, and reasons behind the shift from bewilderment to pride are insufficiently analyzed.

Certain statements are also awkward and do not clearly tie back to the point of the paragraph (e.g., *The narrator mentions their mutual friend, Hollingsworth, and how Zenobia must have been referencing him and others like him living in Blithedale. How they are laughed at by society at large, which would include Zenobia and her current position in society.*).

Sophistication: 1/1

Despite the minor shortcomings in "Evidence and Commentary," the writer nevertheless recognizes and discusses the complexities of the passages in an insightful way throughout the essay, commenting on the evolution of the narrator's feelings and making statements that analyze the conflicting emotions that drive the characters' relationship, e.g., *The imagery of the grand mirror, repeating and doubling this opulence shows Zenobia's figure that is basking in the wealth. The narrator observes how he is shameful of this wealth while Zenobia is prideful in her surroundings, describing to himself her switch of behavior.*

Sample Essay #2

In this dialogue from an 1852 novel by Nathaniel Hawthorne between an unnamed narrator and Zenobia, the narrator's attitude towards Zenobia is exemplified through the narrator's personal thoughts and both direct and indirect characterization of Zenobia. The narrator begins by remarking on how Zenobia's ostentatious manner and self-image is reflected in her room's decor and excessive, even garish, splendor. The narrator's competitive attitude towards Zenobia and her domineering demeanor is evidenced by Hawthorne's use of diction and interrogative tone which is felt as soon as the exchange begins. **The overpowering contempt the narrator exhibits towards Zenobia in both personal, inward opinion and in the challenging questions directed at her show that upon leaving the communal rural lifestyle of Blithedale farm, these two characters see each other as anything but equal, both trying to one-up the other with every chance they get.**

The narrator's description of Zenobia's room is wordy and poetic, bordering on obsessive ranting, not trying to conceal the envy the narrator feels for her in the slightest. Nearly every line in the first paragraph is comparative: "The furniture was exceedingly rich," as compared to their, "old farm-house, with its homely board and benches in the dining-room, and a few wicker chairs in the best parlor," while Zenobia's quarters held "pictures, marbles, vases...more shapes of luxury than there could be any object of enumerating." After leaving a lifestyle where everything was impoverished and even those poor goods communally shared, the narrator feels awestruck at the splendor and luxury that Zenobia commands as her own, with such natural ease and dominance, no less. There is contempt for Zenobia's gaudy displays of wealth, as the narrator, "malevolently beheld the true character of the woman, passionate, luxurious, lacking simplicity, not deeply refined, incapable of pure and perfect taste." Here we are shown the narrator's own values, of the specific kind of modesty which is deemed acceptable, one of which Zenobia has no qualms of foregoing in place of her own self-expression. The narrator flat-out describes their feelings toward Zenobia as "malevolent", clearly they are competitors after having left the Blithedale farm.

However, the next paragraph reveals that while the narrator would not personally choose such a showy display of wealth and individuality, the narrator cannot deny that Zenobia, "gorgeous as she pleased," was able to pull it off herself, that she was able to, "do a thousand things that would have been ridiculous in the poor, thin, weakly characters of other women." Perhaps the narrator sees themselves as possessing such a weakly character. The narrator is hard-pressed to ascertain Zenobia's true nature, is she truly such a flamboyant and graceful creature or is masking something just as weakly, holding up, "the illusion which a great actress flings around her."

As the actual dialogue exchange begins we see that both the narrator and Zenobia are trading verbal jabs at each other, both are clearly aware of the game they are playing, as Zenobia seemingly mocks the narrator for taking the Blithedale farm as a thing of the past and only the past instead of simply another form of the continuous present. The narrator, desperate to find the kink in Zenobia's chain, mentions and disparages Hollingsworth, their mutual friend from the farm who was clearly a sore reminder for Zenobia. When the narrator bluntly insults him, highlighting the waste of his potential on the Blithedale farm,

"Zenobia's eyes darted lightening; her cheeks flushed; the vividness of her expression was like the effect of a powerful light, flaming up suddenly within her." The entire last paragraph continues in a triumphant tone, self-congratulatory as the narrator is proud of wounding the "proud and self-possessed" Zenobia.

From the beginning of the excerpt, the jealous, in-depth description of the Zenobia's room, full of both admiring and simultaneously negative adjectives, to the catty dialogue exchange, and finally the satisfaction of breaking Zenobia's stoicism, the narrator seems to really have it out for Zenobia, perhaps because of the majorly different ways the two characters are coping with the escape from the Blithedale farm. The fact that that narrator's prying question was seen as an, "experiment...finally succeeded," is the final clue that there was, indeed, a toxic competitive spirit between the narrator and Zenobia, with the narrator harboring feelings of envy for Zenobia's circumstances and her bewildering pride and self-possession.

Score: 5/6

Thesis: 1/1

The essay earns a point for the thesis because it presents a defensible, if somewhat convoluted, claim about the narrator's relationship with Zenobia (*The overpowering contempt the narrator exhibits towards Zenobia in both personal, inward opinion and in the challenging questions directed at her show that upon leaving the communal rural lifestyle of Blithedale farm, these two characters see each other as anything but equal, both trying to one-up the other with every chance they get*).

Evidence and Commentary: 3/4

Although the essay does include a number of quotations from the passage, they do not always support the points the writer intends to make. The second paragraph, for example, starts out on solid footing, by citing the many comparisons between Zenobia's room and the old farmhouse as evidence for the idea that the narrator is driven by a need to compete with Zenobia; however, the discussion of the narrator's values and the description of Zenobia as "malevolent," while showing insight, are not fully connected back to the idea of competition. In the following paragraph, the writer also does not make clear the relationship between the narrator's observations of Zenobia and the desire to compete with her. The statement *Perhaps, even, the narrator sees themselves as possessing such a weakly character* hints at the connection, but the idea is not investigated further. **Remember:** if you make a point, you must analyze it!

Sophistication: 1/1

Although the writer does not always effectively connect the evidence from the passage back to the thesis, the essay nevertheless earns the "Sophistication" point because it demonstrates a nuanced understanding of the dynamic between the narrator and Zenobia. Throughout the essay, the writer repeatedly calls attention to the conflicting impulses behind the narrator's reactions, and statements such as *the narrator is hard-pressed to ascertain Zenobia's true nature,* reflect an understanding of the ambiguity of the characters' relationship.

Passage 2 (from *The Rise of Silas Lapham* by William Dean Howells; 2019 exam)

They were not girls who embroidered or abandoned themselves to needle-work. Irene spent her abundant leisure in shopping for herself and her mother, of whom both daughters made a kind of idol, buying her caps and laces out of their pin-money, and getting her dresses far beyond her capacity to wear. Irene dressed herself very stylishly, and spent hours on her toilet every day. Her sister had a simpler taste, and, if she had done altogether as she liked, might even have slighted dress. They all three took long naps every day, and sat hours together minutely discussing what they saw out of the window. In her self-guided search for self-improvement, the elder sister went to many church lectures on a vast variety of secular subjects, and usually came home with a comic account of them, and that made more matter of talk for the whole family. She could make fun of nearly everything; Irene complained that she scared away the young men whom they got acquainted with at the dancing-school sociables. They were, perhaps, not the wisest young men.

The girls had learned to dance at Papanti's; but they had not belonged to the private classes. They did not even know of them, and a great gulf divided them from those who did. Their father did not like company, except such as came informally in their way; and their mother had remained too rustic to know how to attract it in the sophisticated city fashion. None of them had grasped the idea of European travel; but they had gone about to mountain and sea-side resorts, the mother and the two girls, where they witnessed the spectacle which such resorts present throughout New England, of multitudes of girls, lovely, accomplished, exquisitely dressed, humbly glad of the presence of any sort of young man; but the Laphams had no skill or courage to make themselves noticed, far less courted by the solitary invalid, or clergyman, or artist. They lurked helplessly about in the hotel parlors, looking on and not knowing how to put themselves forward. Perhaps they did not care a great deal to do so. They had not a conceit of themselves, but a sort of content in their own ways that one may notice in certain families. The very strength of their mutual affection was a barrier to worldly knowledge; they dressed for one another; they equipped their house for their own satisfaction; they lived richly to themselves, not because they were selfish, but because they did not know how to do otherwise. The elder daughter did not care for society, apparently. The younger, who was but three years younger, was not yet quite old enough to be ambitious of it. With all her wonderful beauty, she had an innocence almost vegetable. When her beauty, which in its immaturity was crude and harsh, suddenly ripened, she bloomed and glowed with the unconsciousness of a flower; she not merely did not feel herself admired, but hardly knew herself discovered. If she dressed well, perhaps too well, it was because she had the instinct of dress; but till she met this young man who was so nice to her at Baie St. Joan, she had scarcely lived a detached, individual life, so wholly had she depended on her mother and her sister for her opinions, almost her sensations. She took account of everything he did and said, pondering it, and trying to make out exactly what he meant, to the inflection of a syllable, the slightest movement or gesture. In this way she began for the first time to form ideas which she had not derived from her family, and they were none the less her own because they were often mistaken.

Sample Essay #3

In the 1885 novel, The Rise of Silas Lapham, **Howells reveals the complex experience of the two sisters within their family and society through the use of details, tone, and juxtaposition of the family with society at large.** Through his writing, he paints a picture of two sisters in a comfortable and tight knit family at the periphery of New England high society. The family is interdependent and content; but towards the end of the passage, independence is sparked in Irene through an encounter with a young man.

Howells uses carefully selected details to offer us a glimpse into the sisters' family lives and relationship with society. He begins by showing the reader details about the sisters which show us their role in the family. "Irene spent her abundant leisure in shopping for herself and her mother..." (4) while "The elder sister went to many church lectures... and usually came home with a comic account of them." (14) These details present the family as caring and amicable, enjoying spending time together. Howells also uses detail to show how the family is on the cusp of high society, yet not fully accepted into it. "The girls had learned to dance at Papanti's; but they had not belonged to the private classes. They did not even know of them..." (22) This crucial distinction reflects the families apathy and ignorance towards the society they border. Near the end of the passage, cracks begin to appear in this ignorance and isolation, as Howells reveals through details in Irene's interaction with the young man: "She took account of everything he did and said, pondering it, and trying to make out exactly what he meant, to the inflection of a syllable..." (64) Although Irene is intrigued by the man, the fact that she cannot grasp his intentions, despite paying close attention to his behavior, emphasizes her innocence and lack of knowledge of the world beyond her close-knit household.

Furthermore, Howells' shifts in tone throughout the passage reinforce the evolving relationship between the three women. For example, at the beginning of the passage, he states, "They all three took long naps every day, and sat hours together minutely discussing what they saw out of the window." (10) Here, Howells uses a languid, homely tone to introduce the sisters' dynamic with their family as intimate and comfortable. Later on in the passage, Howells takes this close knit relationship further, using an singular tone to convey the family's insular nature: "...they dressed for one another; they equipped their house for their own satisfaction; they lived richly to themselves..." (45) Near the end of the passage, however, Howells uses a poetic tone to convey the transformation Irene begins to go through, comparing her to a flower. "When her beauty, which in its immaturity was crude and harsh, suddenly ripened, she bloomed and glowed with the unconsciousness of a flower..." (54) This image of unfolding makes it clear that she is becoming a person far different from the one who spent days lounging with her mother and sister. The lushness of the language emphasizes Irene's metamorphosis.

Lastly, Howells juxtaposes the family next to society to show their peculiarly insular qualities and cluelessness of high society. "...multitudes of girls, lovely, accomplished, exquisitely dressed... but the Laphams had no skill or courage to make themselves noticed." (33) This quote shows how while the Laphams go to the same places as the prominent in society, they lack the knowhow or drive to break into the society. This is magnified in the following quote: "They lurked helplessly about in the hotel parlors, looking on and not knowing how to put themselves forward." (39) By putting the Lapham's right in the middle of high society, Howells draws attention to the family's isolated nature, emphasizing the distance that Irene must travel to become an independent person, as well as the strength of character necessary for her to break away. Even the fact that Irene's ideas were "often mistaken" (line 70) cannot be interpreted as a criticism. Rather, the very fact that she is able to formulate her own ideas testifies to the force of her blossoming independence.

In conclusion, Howells uses details, tone, and juxtaposition to portray two sisters' experience in a closed off family on the edge of society, and how one sister begins to take tentative steps toward breaking away.

Score: 6/6

Thesis: 1/1

This essay earns the "Thesis" point because it opens with a clear and defensible claim (*Howells reveals the complex experience of the two sisters within their family and society through the use of details, tone, and juxtaposition of the family with society at large*).

Note that in this case, the writer essentially rephrases the prompt itself (students were asked to analyze the author's portrayal of the "complex relationship" of Irene and her sister, Penelope, in the context of their family/society) in order to devote maximum time to writing the essay. While this can be a risky strategy, leading to an overly generalized thesis that is difficult to support effectively, the writer makes it work effectively here by establishing upfront the specific techniques by which Howells conveys this relationship, and then devoting a complete paragraph to each one. The presentation of the essay's structure in the introduction allows the reader to feel oriented within the argument from the start.

Evidence and Commentary: 4/4

Each of the body paragraphs makes extensive use of quotations that clearly support the point of the section. Throughout the essay, quotations are consistently commented on and related back to the thesis, e.g., *"The girls had learned to dance at Papanti's; but they had not belonged to the private classes. They did not even know of them..." (22) This crucial distinction reflects the families apathy and ignorance towards the society they border* and *"She took account of everything he did and said, pondering it, and trying to make out exactly what he meant, to the inflection of a syllable..." (64) Although Irene is intrigued by the man, the fact that she cannot grasp his intentions, despite paying close attention to his behavior, emphasizes her innocence and lack of knowledge of the world beyond her close-knit household.*

Notice that this essay is much easier to follow than the previous two. The commentary flows naturally from the quotations and is unobstructed by the kind of distractingly flowery language found in the other essays. As a result, the reader is free to focus on the writer's ideas.

That is not to say that the analysis is flawless. In the third paragraph, for example, it is not entirely clear what the writer means by a "singular" tone; however, this minor issue is outweighed by the strength of the overall analysis.

Sophistication: 1/1

The essay earns the "Sophistication" point because it effectively explores the tension between the insular, self-focused Latham women and the larger society from which they are largely excluded, as well as the significance of Irene's first cautious step toward breaking away from her family and establishing her independence. At each point, the discussion is centered on a specific technique, e.g., *Near the end of the passage, however, Howells uses a poetic tone to convey the transformation Irene begins to go through, comparing her to a flower. "When her beauty, which in its immaturity was crude and harsh, suddenly ripened, she bloomed and glowed with the unconsciousness of a flower..." (54) This image of unfolding makes it clear that she is becoming a person far different from the one who spent days lounging with her mother and sister. The lushness of the language emphasizes Irene's metamorphosis.*

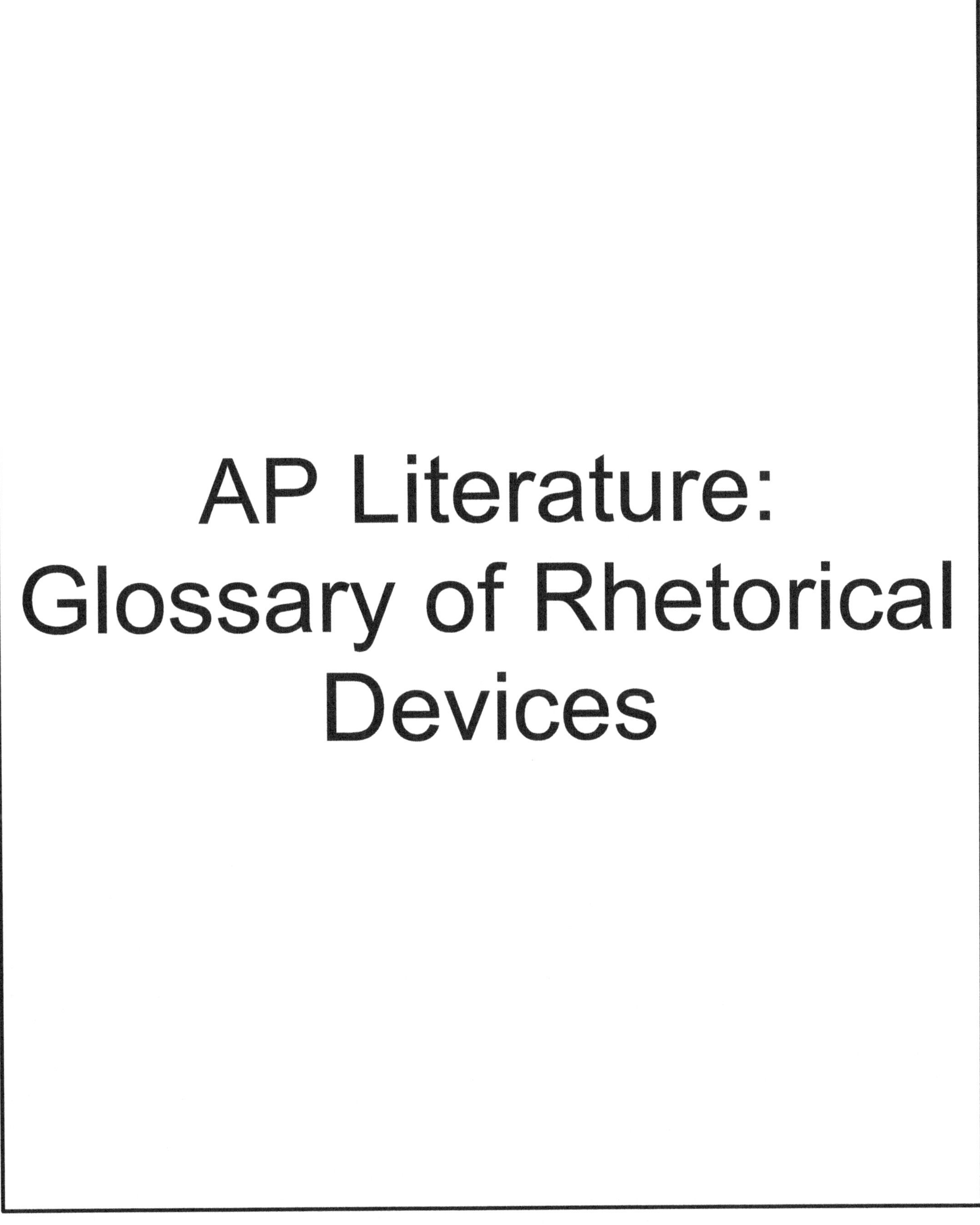

AP Literature: Glossary of Rhetorical Devices

Glossary

Literary and Figurative Language

Abstract Language – vague and generalized speech, full of references to intangible concepts.

Example: She felt a **tremulous need** to throw her **liberty** and her **leisure** into the things of the **soul**—the **most beautiful things** she knew. She found them, when she gave time to seeking, in a hundred places, and particularly in a **dim and sacred region**—the region of **active pity**—over her entrance into which she dropped curtains so thick that it would have been an impertinence to lift them.

Allusion – (Indirect) reference, usually to a literary/artistic work, character, or event

Example: Imogen saw a woman of immense stature, in a very short skirt and a broad, flapping sun hat, striding down the hillside at a long, swinging gait. The refugee from **Valhalla** approached, panting. Her heavy, Teutonic features were scarlet from the rigor of her exercise, and her hair, under her flapping sun hat, was tightly befrizzled about her brow.

In Norse mythology, Valhalla was a great hall ruled over by the gods, where slain warriors were sent after falling in combat. Note that if a passage contains a reference that high school students are not expected to know, a footnote will generally be provided.

Aside – Parenthetical remark used to offer commentary or address the reader directly.

Shortcut: Parentheses and dashes

Example: Mary and I were brought up in the strictest seclusion. My mother, being at once highly accomplished, well informed, and fond of employment, took the whole charge of our education on herself, with the exception of Latin—**which my father undertook to teach us**—so that we never even went to school; and, as there was no society in the neighbourhood, our only intercourse with the world consisted in a stately tea-party, now and then, with the principal farmers and tradespeople of the vicinity **(just to avoid being stigmatized as too proud to consort with our neighbours)**, and an annual visit to our paternal grandfather.

Cliché – Trite saying that expresses a common or banal idea.

Examples: A troop of newly arrived students, very young, pink and callow, followed nervously, rather abjectly, at the Director's heels. Each of them carried a notebook, in which, whenever the great man spoke, he desperately scribbled. **Straight from the horse's mouth.** It was a rare privilege.

Dry/Wry Humor, Irony – Form of subtle, sometimes dark, humor, frequently based on wordplay or violation of the reader's expectations.

> **Example:** Being pretty well aware of what sort of **joy** you must both be feeling, I have been in no hurry with my congratulations; but I hope it all went off tolerably well. How did you all behave? **Who cried most?**

In most cases, one does not ask people feeling joy about how much they cried. Although the example above is taken from a discussion of a wedding—a happy event at which people do often cry—the unexpected juxtaposition between a positive emotion and a response typically associated with sadness creates a humorous moment.

Euphemism – Replacement of an offensive, crass, or unpleasant word with a milder one.

> **Example:** The good old office, now extinct in the State of New-York, of a Master in Chancery, had been conferred upon me. It was not a very arduous office, but very **pleasantly remunerative**.

Here, the narrator uses the refined phrase *pleasantly remunerative* as a roundabout way of indicating that he earns a lot of money.

Imagery – Rich, descriptive language that appeals to the senses.

> **Example:** The sun shone with a warm yellow light on the Upper Town, with its girdle of gray wall, and on the red flag that drowsed above the citadel, and was a friendly lustre on the tinned roofs of the Lower Town; while away off to the south and east and west wandered the purple hills and the farmlit plains in such dewy shadow and effulgence as would have been enough to make the heaviest heart glad.

Hyperbole (Exaggeration) – Overstated or over-the-top language employed for dramatic or humorous effect.

> **Example:** She moped: **no grown person** could have performed that uncheering business better; **no furrowed face** of adult exile, longing for Europe at Europe's antipodes, **ever** bore more legibly the signs of homesickness than did her infant visage.

Metaphor – Comparison that does not state that *x is like/as y*, but rather than *x* <u>*is*</u> *y*.

> **Example:** For a few moments **I was turned into a pillar of salt**, standing at the head of my seated column of clerks.

Metonymy – Replacement of a literal word or phrase by a closely related one.

> **Example:** While Captain Delano was thus made the mark of all eager **tongues**, his one eager glance took in all faces, with every other object about him.

Pathos (Appeal to Emotion) – Use of strong or highly charged language to elicit an emotional response.

Example: What an excellent example of the power of dress, young Oliver Twist was! Wrapped in the blanket which had hitherto formed his only covering, he might have been the child of a nobleman or a beggar; it would have been hard for the haughtiest stranger to have assigned him his proper station in society. But now that he was enveloped in the old calico robes which had grown yellow in the same service, he was badged and ticketed, and fell into his place at once—a parish child—the orphan of a workhouse—**the humble, half-starved drudge—to be cuffed and buffeted through the world—despised by all, and pitied by none**.

Personification – Attribution of human characteristics to an inanimate object.

Example: **Five-fingered** ferns hung over the water and dropped spray from their fingertips... The high mountain wind coasted, **sighing** through the pass and **whistled** on the edges of the big blocks of broken granite.

Rhetorical Question – Question asked without expectation of response, usually for dramatic effect or to emphasize a point.

Example: I stood gazing at him awhile, as he went on with his own writing, and then reseated myself at my desk. This is very strange, thought I. **What had one best do?**

Speculation – Wonder about, come up with a possible explanation for

Shortcut: Maybe, perhaps, question marks

Example: As the train neared Tarrytown, Imogen Willard began to wonder why she had consented to be one of Flavia's house party at all. She had not felt enthusiastic about it since leaving the city, and was experiencing a prolonged ebb of purpose, a current of chilling indecision, under which she vainly sought for the motive which had induced her to accept Flavia's invitation. **Perhaps** it was a vague curiosity to see Flavia's husband, who had been the magician of her childhood and the hero of innumerable Arabian fairy tales. **Perhaps** it was a desire to see M. Roux, whom Flavia had announced as the especial attraction of the occasion. **Perhaps** it was a wish to study that remarkable woman in her own setting.

Synecdoche – Use of the part to represent the whole.

Example: The enormous room on the ground floor faced towards the north. Cold for all the summer beyond the **panes**, for all the tropical heat of the room itself, a harsh thin light glared through the windows, hungrily seeking some draped lay figure, some pallid shape of academic goose-flesh, but finding only the glass and nickel and bleakly shining porcelain of a laboratory.

In the above example, the word *panes* is used as a stand-in for *windows*.

Understatement (Litotes) – Use of excessively restrained language. Opposite of hyperbole.

This is a form of irony and dry/wry humor, often used to satirize or mock.

Example: [T]he civilest...of men in the morning, yet in the afternoon he was disposed, upon provocation, to be **slightly rash** with his tongue, in fact, insolent.

The word *insolent* (extremely rude) at the end of the sentence indicates that the individual in question was much more than "slightly" rash.

Wordplay – Verbal wit or punning, often involving double meanings of words.

Example: They seemed to think the opportunity lost, if they failed to **point** the conversation to me, every now and then, and stick the **point** into me.

Comparing and Contrasting

Antithesis – Use of parallel structure to set opposing ideas in contrast to one another.

Example: Winter and summer, then, were two hostile lives, and bred two separate natures. **Winter was always the effort to live; summer was tropical license**.

Comparison – Description of the similarities between two people or things.

Example: Marianne's abilities were, in many respects, **quite equal** to Elinor's. She was sensible and clever; but eager in everything: her sorrows, her joys, could have no moderation. She was generous, amiable, interesting: she was everything but prudent. The **resemblance** between her and her mother was strikingly great.

Contrast, or Juxtaposition – Description of opposing qualities.

Example: ...beyond [the den] was the **luxurious bathroom, a modern miracle of enamel tiling and shining glass**. Across the sun-flooded back of the house [was] Alice's little bedroom, **nunlike in its rigid austerity**.

Extended Analogy is an analogy that continues beyond a single comparison, lasting for several sentences or even a paragraph.

Example: At first Bartleby did an extraordinary quantity of writing. As if long **famishing** for something to copy, he seemed to **gorge himself** on my documents. There was no pause for **digestion**. He ran a day and night line, copying by sun-light and by candle-light.

Oxymoron – Two contradictory terms placed next to one another for contrast.

Example: Parting is such **sweet sorrow**.

Paradox – Statement or situation that appears illogical or contradictory but that may reveal an underlying truth.

Example: There was only one catch and that was Catch-22, which specified that a concern for one's own safety in the face of dangers that were real and immediate was the process of a rational mind. Orr was crazy and could be grounded. All he had to do was ask; and as soon as he did, he would no longer be crazy and would have to fly more missions.

Simile – Comparison using *like* or *as*.

Example: In the morning, one might say, his face was of a fine florid hue, but after twelve o'clock, meridian—his dinner hour—**it blazed <u>like</u> a grate full of Christmas coals**.

Repetition

Alliteration – Repetition of the same sound at the beginnings of multiple words.

Example: [H]alf-a-dozen **four-footed fiends**, of various sizes and ages, issued from hidden dens to the common centre.

Anadiplosis – Repetition of a word at the end of one statement and the beginning of the following one.

Example: For me it is a misfortune. A misfortune, everyone knows what that is…

Anaphora – Repetition of a word or phrase at the beginning of a series of consecutive sentences/parts of a sentence.

Example: [H]e **had** stolen away from every one alike, **had** kept no appointment and renewed no acquaintance, **had** been indifferently aware of the number of persons who esteemed themselves fortunate in being, unlike himself, "met," and **had** even independently, unsociably, alone… given his afternoon and evening to the immediate and the sensible.

Assonance – Repetition of a vowel sound within a group of words.

Example: The spider skins l**ie** on their s**i**des, translucent and ragged…

Parallel Structure – Repetition of the same construction with a sentence or paragraph.

Example: He had spent some such good hours there, had forgotten, in her warm, golden drawing-room, **<u>so much of the</u> loneliness** and **<u>so many of the</u> worries of his life**, that it had come to be **<u>the immediate answer</u> to his longings, <u>the cure</u> for his aches, <u>the harbour</u> of refuge from his storms**.

Polysyndeton – Repeated use of a conjunction to join multiple clauses or parts of a sentence.

Example: It was four o'clock in the afternoon **and** the kitchen was square **and** gray **and** quiet.

Answers: Thesis Quick Check

1. 0 points
2. 0 points
3. 1 point
4. 0 points
5. 1 point

Recommended Resources

All of the AP English essay prompts since 1999, along with sample responses and scoring analyses, can be found on the AP Central section of the College Board website:

https://apcentral.collegeboard.org/courses/ap-english-language-and-composition/exam?course=ap-english-language-and-composition

https://apcentral.collegeboard.org/courses/ap-english-literature-and-composition/exam.

Main Works Cited

Hawthorne, Nathaniel. *The Blithedale Romance*, 1852. http://www.online-literature.com/hawthorne/blithedale_romance/

Howells, William Dean. *The Rise of Silas Lapham*, 1885. http://www.online-literature.com/william-dean-howells/silas-lapham/

Marshall, George C. Speech delivered at Harvard University, 1947. https://www.marshallfoundation.org/marshall/the-marshall-plan/marshall-plan-speech/

Wharton, Edith. *The House of Mirth*, 1905. http://www.online-literature.com/wharton/house_mirth/

About the Author

Erica Meltzer earned her B.A., *magna cum laude*, from Wellesley College and spent more than a decade tutoring privately in Boston and New York City, as well as nationally and internationally online. Her experience working with students from a wide range of educational backgrounds and virtually every score level gave her unique insight into the types of stumbling blocks students often encounter while preparing for standardized reading and writing tests.

She was inspired to begin writing her own test-prep materials in 2007, after visiting a local bookstore in search of additional practice questions for an SAT Writing student. Unable to find material that replicated the contents of the exam with sufficient accuracy, she decided to write her own. What started as a handful of exercises jotted down on a piece of paper became the basis for her first book, the original *Ultimate Guide to SAT® Grammar*, published in 2011. Since that time, she has authored guides for SAT reading and vocabulary, as well as verbal guides for the ACT®, GRE®, and GMAT®. Her books have sold well over 100,000 copies and are used by students around the world. She lives in New York City, and you can visit her online at www.thecriticalreader.com.

Made in the USA
Coppell, TX
01 June 2020

26822533R00063